TAC Fighters

Robert F. Dorr and Jim Benson

Motorbooks International
Publishers & Wholesalers ®

First published in 1991 by Motorbooks International Publishers & Wholesalers, P O Box 2, 729 Prospect Avenue, Osceola, WI 54020 USA

Motorbooks International books are also available at discounts in bulk quantity for industrial or sales-promotional use. For details write to Special Sales Manager at the Publisher's address

Library of Congress Cataloging-in-Publication Data
Dorr, Robert F.
    TAC fighters / Robert F. Dorr, Jim Benson.
        p. cm.
    ISBN 0-87938-507-3
    1. Fighter planes—United States.
2. United States. Air Force. Tactical Air Command. I. Benson, Jim. II. Title.
UB1242.F5D66   1991
358.4'383'0973—dc20   90-26589

On the front cover: F-15A Eagle fighters of the 142nd Fighter-Interceptor Group, Portland, Oregon, crackle through a cloud-laced sky along the cold Pacific coastline on 31 January 1990. The sideways slit directly behind the pilot is a cooling air exhaust duct for the cockpit air-conditioning system and is flanked, atop the two engines, by intake bypass air spill ducts while helping regulate the flow of air into the jet engines. Radar warning receiver (RWR) aerial atop the Eagle's left vertical fin (at right in picture) gives the fin a different tip shape than the fin on the right, which has an electronic countermeasures aerial on top. The Portland group has an air defense assignment. *Jim Benson*

On the back cover: The wall located behind F-4E Phantom 68-0351, starting up engines in St. Louis on 30 January 1990, shows how cramped space is for Missouri Air National Guardsman. Aircraft 68-0351 is one of only two Phantoms in US inventory (plus four understood to be in Israeli service) with a one-piece windshield—proposed in the mid 1980s as one of several possible upgrade features for the entire fleet. The crew will not go anywhere in this jet until red tags are removed. *Robert F. Dorr*

On the frontispiece: F-4C Phantom 63-7530 banks over seasonally pristine Pacific Northwest territory on 3 August 1989. Before converting to the F-15A Eagle, the Portland-based 142nd Fighter-Interceptor Group operated the Phantom and included in its inventory a couple of F-4Cs that had downed MiGs in Vietnam. The Air Defense Gray paint scheme, which includes a coat of paint over the Phantom's radome, is different from the more recent Hill Gray Two in which other squadrons' Phantoms have been painted, and allows for larger national insignia as well as "US AIR FORCE" lettering. *Jim Benson*

On the title page: They call it the (bleep) jet in a certain city where a manufacturer of other fighters has its factory, but to most of the world the F-16 Fighting Falcon is the most exciting fighter that has come along in a generation. Maj. Mark Meyer of the Montana Air National Guard pilots F-16A 80-0565, callsign BULLET 02, over his home neighborhood on 18 August 1989. Launch rail for Sidewinder missile at right wingtip is empty and F-16A is in "clean" condition except for 300 gallon centerline drop tank. *Jim Benson*

Printed and bound in Singapore by PH Productions

Contents

When the F-16 first appeared, its fuselage configuration with the engine intake below and behind the pilot seemed odd, and no claim was made for gracefulness. Now that we're used to it, the Electric Jet—so nicknamed for its fly-by-wire controls—looks exactly like we think it should look. Seen in April 1988, aircraft 83-1119 is an F-16C belonging to the 6512nd Test Squadron, part of the Air Force Flight Test Center at Edwards AFB, California. *Carl E. Porter*

Acknowledgments

Even a modest look at the Tactical Air Command's fighter force (including its "TAC-gained" Air National Guard and Air Force Reserve components) would have been impossible without assistance from many people. Any errors are the sole responsibility of the authors, but if there should be any credit, it belongs to many in and out of Tactical Air who made this work possible.

Assistance in the preparation of this work was provided by the Department of Defense, Headquarters United States Air Force, Headquarters Tactical Air Command, the National Guard Bureau and numerous Tactical Air fast fighter bases. The authors owe a very special debt to Maj. Brian C. Rogers, who yanks and banks in nothing with a wing span of less than 185 feet and who gave generously of his photography and expertise.

General Dynamics Corporation, builder of the Viper, generously allowed us to use material in its support digest, *Code One,* and we are indebted to Al Spivak, Joe Sutherland, Joe Stout and Joe Thornton. McDonnell Aircraft Company, builder of Phantoms and Eagles, provided a plant tour and simulator ride, for which we thank Tim Beecher, Burt Bacheller, Tom Downey, Kim Kitson and Jenny Horton.

We also want to acknowledge our debt to the following:

At Andrews AFB, Maryland: Brig. Gen. Russell Davis, Lt. Col. Harold (Hobie) Hobart, Lt. Col. David Wherley, Lt. Col. Vince Shiban, 1LT Gerald McManus, TSGT Eunice Graham.

At Fairchild AFB, Washington: Col. Wayne Engstrom, Col. Walt Hodgen, Capt. Bill Young, TSGT Ike Isaacson, TSGT Bruce Olsen, TSGT Dan Moriarty.

At Great Falls, Montana: Lt. Col. Don Stevlingson, Lt. Col. Rex Tanberg, Lt. Col. Joe Erickson, Maj. Mark Meyer, Maj. Mike Milburn, Maj. Jim Burman, Capt. Ray Lynn, 1LT Bryan Fox, MSGT Verne Pankratz, TSGT George DeShaw, TSGT Harvey Hall, TSGT Ron Halverson.

At Langley AFB, Virginia: Capt. Tom Christie.

At Malmstrom AFB, Montana: Capt. Rae Smolen, Lt. Robyn Chumley.

At McChord AFB, Washington: Capt. Theresa Gates.

At Mountain Home AFB, Idaho: Col. Arnie Franklin, Capt. Steve Salmonson, Capt. Bill Brunner.

In the Pentagon: Lt. Col. James Ragan, Maj. Richard M. (Dick) Cole, John Hoffman, Don Black.

At Portland, Oregon: Maj. Lyle Cabe, TSGT Ken Coats, Maj. Matt Skundrick.

Among the fraternity: Robert S. (Beaver) Blake, David F. Brown, Thomas F. (Frank) Evans, Greg Field, Robert B. Greby, Joseph G. Handelman, DDS, Fred Harl, Barbara Harold, John J. Harty, M. J. Kasiuba, Mary La Barre, Don Linn, Don Logan, Peter Mancus, Donald S. McGarry, David W. Menard, R. J. Mills, Jr., Tim Parker, Robert A. Pfannenschmidt, Carl E. Porter, "the gang at Roy's," Bill Strandberg and Arnold Swanberg.

Electric Jet

You're going up to fight. You're number two in RAMBO Flight, a two-ship fighter formation. It's a cloudless, sun-baked day and you're the pilot of a jet that is—there is no other word—awesome.

Call it the Lawn Dart. The Viper. The Electric Jet. According to the brochure it's the F–16 Fighting Falcon.

It's also the backbone of Tactical Air's fighter force. This is the fighter team celebrated on these pages. It includes Tactical Air Command (TAC) and TAC-gained Air National Guard and Reserve squadrons.

Fighters in this team also include the F–4 Phantom and F–15 Eagle. But the F–16 Lawn Dart stands out. To younger pilots, the F–16 is what a fighter should look like. To older pilots, who *know* what a fighter should look like, the F–16 is funny-looking and funny-acting. It's stalky, with a low-slung, hungry-looking air intake, and it has a peculiar canopy, cockpit, flight controls and warmaking gadgetry.

Fighters, to use the classic meaning of the word, and to state plainly what this book is about, shoot down airplanes. On these pages you'll go air-to-air: snap on your G-suit, tighten up the Koch fittings of your harness, grab your new, lightweight helmet and go out to shoot down the enemy in his aircraft. To paraphrase actor Robert Prosky in his now-defunct *Hill Street Blues* role, you're

going to do it to him before he can do it to you.

World War I air ace Baron Manfred Von Richthofen summarized the air-to-air combat mission: "The fighter pilots have to rove in the area allotted to them in any way they like, and when they spot an enemy they attack and shoot him down. Anything else is rubbish."

Von Richthofen never heard of a HUD (head-up display), of fly-by-wire controls or of missiles, MiGs or sidesticks, but his fabric-covered biplane with its manual machine gun did the same job as today's glass-cockpit Electric Jet.

So, you've been in the ready room and briefed with your flight leader, RAMBO 01. Today's mission is to engage MiG-29s—more correctly, Navy Tomcats behaving like MiGs.

Now, you get a weather brief in Operations and head for your plane.

F–16A Fighting Falcons on final approach for Great Falls Airport, Montana, on 18 August 1989. Aircraft 81-0665, callsign BULLET 02, is in the hands of Maj. Mike Milburn, who has previously instructed in the T–38 Talon and flown the C–141 Starlifter. Plane 80-0565, callsign BULLET 01, is piloted by Maj. Mark Meyer, who was one of the first pilots of the 120th Fighter-Interceptor Squadron to upgrade from the F–106A Delta Dart to the F–16A and is an instructor in the latter. Montana's are "block 30" (F–16A–30–CF) aircraft with slightly larger horizontal tail surfaces than later F–16A and F–16C models. *Jim Benson*

If there exists anything more beautiful than this Tactical Air Command F-16B belonging to the Thunderbirds flight demonstration team, we don't know what it is. The 'birds operate two of these two-seat models, currently numbers 80-638 and 81-815, but since their ship number 8 is painted with a lacquer-based paint that can be wiped on and off at will, the B model in this photo may not be either 80-638 or 81-815. *Jim Benson*

Posed recruiting shots depict the heat and frenzy of a fighter scramble with pilots racing furiously toward their jets. In real life, you reach your F-16 by riding a large blue bus.

The first thing you notice about your waiting F-16 is the low-slung air intake for its 24,670 lb. thrust F100 turbofan engine. Later models use either F100 or F110. Being close to the ground, that intake has tried to suck up a maintenance person or two but has so far devoured only headphones and the occasional ballpoint pen.

On later-model F-16s, the canopy has an amber tint because of its gold radar-absorbing materials (RAM)—not just gold-colored, but actual gold. Other kinds of RAM cover the area around the air intake.

Except for a small portion at the very rear, the F-16 Viper's canopy is a one-piece teardrop. Because the single-piece structure affords spectacular, all-around visibility, it's exactly what the fighter pilot has always wanted—and what the engineers said could never be built.

A gaggle of F-16s on the line at Luke Air Force Base, Arizona, on 12 January 1989, with two-seat F-16D 86-1040 in the rear. F-16C and D models can be distinguished externally from F-16A and B models by the blade antenna for a UHF radio located forward on the fairing at the base of the vertical tail. These late-model Vipers are flown by the Air Force Reserve's 944th Tactical Fighter Group. *Robert B. Greby*

So climb aboard. This is not easy to do. With the exception of the front seat in the Army's AH-64 Apache, the F-16 is probably the most difficult aircraft in the American arsenal to swing your legs into. No one denies this: test pilot Tim D. Eason likens the F-16 to the Jaguar XKE V-12, saying (in the manufacturer's publication, *Code One*), "They both look like they're going Mach 2 standing still. They're both hard to get into and out of."

Once inside, your F-16 Fighting Falcon's cockpit is spacious, comfortable. The cockpit is set up for HOTAS—alphabet soup for "hands on throttle and stick"—which enables the pilot to keep his head up to eyeball MiGs instead of being distracted bending down to scour his instrument panel. He reads instruments peering straight ahead into his personal videogame, the head-up display, and controlling his aircraft by feel with switches and buttons on the side-mounted control stick.

The F-16 ejection seat cants back like your swimming pool lounge chair. It all has to do with the force of gravity (G forces), the F-16 being at least a 9 G aircraft and able, itself, to endure more Gs than your mortal body can. The thirty-degree tilt, along with the raised foot position, can add

Montana's 80-0565 and 81-0751 over Big Sky Country—Flathead Lake, to be specific—during the 18 August 1989 simulated combat mission flown by coauthor Jim Benson. Here, 751 is being flown by Capt. Ray Lynn. Gun port for the F-16A's M61A1 rotary cannon with 515 rounds is located on left fuselage just behind pilot and beneath red triangle with rescue instructions. These F-16As have cannon and wingtip-mounted Sidewinder infrared missiles but are not equipped with the AIM-7 Sparrow radar-guided missile carried by "block 15" airplanes in the F-16A (F-16A-15-CF) series, which have been designated AD F-16A (for air defense). *Jim Benson*

F-16A Fighting Falcon 80–0537 of the 56th Tactical Fighter Wing, with an MC tail code for its home base at MacDill AFB, Florida, is seen during a visit to Great Falls, Montana, in October 1986. As originally delivered, early F-16A models have a smooth leading edge on the vertical fin as shown here, while later F-16A through F-16D aircraft have a small pitot antenna located three-quarters of the way up the leading edge of the fin. *Jim Benson*

at least 1 G to a pilot's personal G tolerance. In the tilted seat, the effect of the G-force is reduced and the pilot has a lesser prospect of suffering G-LOC (gravity induced loss of consciousness), an affliction which, at high speed and low altitude, can kill.

Which makes it a good time to point out that today's fighter pilot no longer fits the whiskey-drinking, bar-fighting, trouble-prone stereotype of

the past. Booze and high-G fighter combat don't mix. The Air Force discourages abuse of the demon rum. Today's fighter pilot is likely to be squeaky-clean and clearheaded with a weakness for nothing more damaging than a Caesar salad.

OK, so you're strapped in. You're fired up. Your flight leader gets clearance to taxi. RAMBO 01 flexes on his nosewheel and starts out. He

When the TAC-gained District of
Columbia Air National Guard received its
F-16As in September 1989, a suitably
patriotic shot was taken with the
American flag in the background—
correctly displayed, with blue field at
upper left. The one-piece windshield,
emphasized in this front-on view, provides
excellent visibility. Prominent red tags are
attached to protective covers which must
be removed from antennas and pitot tubes
before aircraft is flown. *DC ANG/Thomas
F. Evans*

turns smoothly on the taxi strip. At the controls of RAMBO 02, you follow—impressed with handling and visibility. *Now* you can appreciate that the F-16 seat is positioned very high relative to the canopy/fuselage join, giving superb visibility on the ground and in the air.

Time for takeoff: you let off the brakes, put it in burner, start down the runway and get lift to go up.

There is concern about the lack of pilot cues in the F-16. The stick is oddly placed, on the right side, which according to some makes it harder for right-handed pilots to fly the ship. Since the aircraft trims itself automatically, the pilot rarely has to adjust trim—so he rarely gets the subconscious cue that his air speed has changed. Likewise, the absence of a canopy bow means that the pilot is less likely to hear wind noise—another cue to speed changes.

The enormous power of the engine lifts the F-16 Fighting Falcon from the runway. The aircraft is extremely responsive to its controls. They're called "fly-by-wire" (a feature not found on the F-4 or F-15) because your touch moves flight surfaces with electrical impulses rather than hydraulic-mechanical linkages, hence the Electric Jet sobriquet.

You have a spectacular view of airfield, highways and mere mortals in mid-rush-hour traffic, looking out from your high perch with nothing to obstruct vision.

The engineers were wrong about the one-piece canopy. It gives you a spectacular view. Many combat missions must be flown at low altitude to foil the enemy detection, so they built the canopy to withstand that nemesis of the fighter pilot—the birdstrike.

Wally Perez is employed by General Dynamics to use a 40 ft. stainless-steel gun "barrel" to shoot a 4 lb. chicken at a speed of 350 knots into an F-16 canopy frame bolted securely to the ground. Wally's chicken-shooting exercise is proof enough that the F-16's one-piece canopy isn't going to fail (short of flying into a cinder block in mid-air). But if it did, the combiner glass of the HUD would act as a windshield to protect the pilot.

Here's how one pilot describes the "straight up" takeoff, ideal in communities where jet noise is an issue:

"I'm at the end of the runway ready to take off. I'm finished with the 'last chance' visual checks. My ship is in tiptop condition, the tower clears me, and I go. I put in burner. I let off the brakes. I take off and climb straight up to ten thousand feet without ever crossing the fence around the airport."

Straight up? As recently as the heyday of the F-4 Phantom—no longer spritely, but still included in our TAC, Guard and Reserve force—this would have been science-fiction. But the F-16 can fly straight up. It's among the first generation of fighters that can *sustain* vertical flight and even *accelerate* while climbing straight up. But caution is advised. The F100 and F110 engines used by the F-16 are rated at 25,000 lb. thrust but that's under ideal conditions, at certain temperatures. Apart from routine "fudge factors," experts superimpose a

In a spectacular flyby of the two principal aircraft operated by the District of Columbia Air National Guard, C-22B 83-4615 (a former 727-035 jetliner once operated by National and Pan American airlines), piloted by Maj. Mark Hetterman, lingers in the background on 18 November 1989. Up front, early-model F-16A 85-0520 with Lt. Col. Vince Shiban at the controls is emblazoned with "113 TFW," to denote its role as the aircraft of wing commander Brig. Gen. Russell C. Davis. *Robert F. Dorr*

nominal three percent per thousand feet lapse rate on the remaining thrust, meaning that when you *do* reach 10,000 feet you're operating at seventy percent of peak. So, yes, you *can* fly it straight up—and this does make friends in the community—but prudence is advised.

Today, you take your F-16 up to 33,000 feet, peel out of the departure area and head out to sea. RAMBO 01 takes up station high on your left wing. Flying formation in a jet fighter, you get the optical illusion that you're bobbing up and down when, in fact, you're flying straight along. You tuck in below and behind 01. There is the usual chatter about departure point, altitude, radio frequency. "RAMBO 01 is on," your leader says.

"RAMBO 02's on," you confirm.

Today, the enemy is not a MiG but a pair of Navy F-14 Tomcats. These "pretend" MiGs, the Tomcats, are piloted by clones of actor Tom Cruise, (star of *Top Gun*) who will "kill" you from a distance if they can—or close in, to "yank and bank" in a dogfight with you, if they have to. They're tough, aggressive, smart.

You head on down to the range, a square over the Atlantic where ACM (air combat maneuvering) is practiced. In cruise, the F-16 floats like a ping-pong ball on a liquid surface, almost *too* easy to fly. With your head up—the HOTAS concept, remember—you're peering into your HUD at symbology that winks at you with facts about your flight, including what your APG-66A multimode radar is doing. Early radars produced a direct picture of what they saw. You're looking, instead, at symbology based on what the radar sees. And—Robert Prosky again—you want to see them before they see you.

Here it comes—a two-on-two contest with the Tomcats.

"Fight's on," RAMBO 01 calls. The two F-14 Tomcats, callsigns GYPSY 201 and GYPSY 202, appear from nowhere intent on taking you out. RAMBO 01 is painting the Tomcats on his radar and following them on his HUD, without ever lowering his gaze. "Fight's on, camera on."

The onrushing enemy—GYPSY 201 and GYPSY 202—have contact. Your radar warning receiver (RWR) tells you the Tomcats have you lit up like a Christmas tree.

RAMBO 01 knows you're in the trouble zone. He isn't. Intent on deception, he has prevented the Tomcats from noticing him. "They don't have me," RAMBO 01 says.

The two Tomcats—so your radar tells you—split, bank and come at you in a pincers-style approach at high speed and at a distance, now, of twenty miles. They'll try to out-think you, lock you up and get you with a missile. If GYPSY 201 has his way, he'll do it before you even see each other. It's called BVR, beyond visual range. And the Tomcat has a radar-guided missile, a missile not carried by your F-16 today.

"You have the lead," RAMBO 01 tells you. He wants to stay out of view of the Tomcats, let them focus on you.

"EID hostile," you hear GYPSY 201 call. They've done an electronic ID check and deemed you the enemy. You're thinking of their missiles rushing at you, so you go into a series of high-G defensive maneuvers, taking advantage of the F-16's superior maneuvering capability, to try to break their radar lock-on.

"They're closing at oh-four-zero now," RAMBO 01 says.

"I got 'em. They're coming," you reply.

"They're spreading out, they're spreading out!" declares RAMBO 01. Your flight leader wants to do the same. You ease your right-hand sidestick to the right and create an even greater expanse of open sky between RAMBO 01 and RAMBO 02. This is the critical moment: the Tomcats may be about to shoot you in the face with a radar-guided missile.

"He's locking you up! Break left!" warns RAMBO 01.

You haul the stick to the left, feel the kick of your airplane rising and banking beneath you, and go plunging away at an angle. Had the Tomcats fired a real Phoenix or Sparrow, the missile would now be struggling to follow you in the dive.

Today—this is practice—real missiles aren't being fired but are being simulated electronically. And this time, you outfoxed them. Either GYPSY 201 and GYPSY 202 didn't fire their radar missiles in time, or their missiles were defeated when you went into the break.

Now, the Tomcats face you in a close-up slugfest. "Getting in the telephone booth with the other guy," some call it. This makes almost any other fighter meat on the table for the F-16. You've got them focused with your Mark One Eyeball now, up there on the horizon, and in almost any situation at visual range, you're faster, more maneuverable, deadlier.

And they don't see RAMBO 01 at all!

Prominent in this view of Shiban stalking Hetterman is the Electric Jet's 300 US gallon drop tank, hanging from the centerline and tucked between ventral fins. Ground clearance for the tank during takeoff roll and landing is of such narrow tolerance that before the tank's shape was finalized, a COMOK (computerized mock-up) and the science of kinematics—substituting for costly hardware and wind tunnel work—were used to simulate takeoffs and landings. It was determined that the drop tank would not scrape the runway during a normal landing, a landing with a bounce or a landing with flat tires. In fact, appearances are deceiving: in a mishap, it is more likely the ventral fins or speed brakes would be scraped first. *Robert F. Dorr*

Your F-16 doesn't have a Phoenix or Sparrow, although the Air Defense Fighter (ADF) F-16A *does* carry the latter, but you have plenty to fight with.

To outfight the onrushing Tomcats—or kill a MiG, or shoot down an encroaching bomber of *Sovietskaya Dal'naya Aviatsiya* (Soviet Long-Range Aviation)—your F-16 is simply a conglomeration of steel, titanium, plastic and composites, thrown together for the sole purpose of carrying aloft two AIM-9M Sidewinder heat-seeking air-to-air missiles moored on its wingtips, and one 20 mm M61A1 cannon with 515 rounds mounted in the left forward fuselage immediately aft of the pilot. Take away Sidewinders and gun, and this machine—this conglomeration—has no more purpose than a Rube Goldberg contraption.

The Sidewinder can "reach out and touch someone" at eleven miles (17.7 km), although it's normally used for fighting at closer range. The cannon can shoot down an opponent perhaps 800 yards away.

Your own voice sounds raspy. "RAMBO 02's contact now at oh-five-zero, sixteen miles. Closing."

Even when you can see the Tomcats, it's equally effective to look into the HUD at the radar information when you're trying to get them boxed up—surrounded by the "box" on the symbology which is the modern-day equivalent of having them in your gunsight.

F-16A 81-0674 of the Montana Air National Guard passes in review at Great Falls in April 1988. While an AIM-9M Sidewinder missile is present as usual on the right wingtip, the left wingtip launch rail is noticeably empty indicating that a missile was fired or, more likely in this era when a "shoot" costs $900,000 or more, simply not carried aloft to begin with. *Jim Benson*

"I've got mine," RAMBO 01 says.

The infrared sensor at the tip of your Sidewinder missile gives you an "audible," a tone in your earphones saying the missile has locked on. You fire your missile—today, as a simulation only—at Tomcat number one high to your right. RAMBO 01 slashes across the left quadrant of the sky and picks off Tomcat number two with his gun.

"Got him!" says RAMBO 01.

GYPSY 201 and GYPSY 202 are "dead."

It is not easy to defeat the Tomcat, with its superb radar, missiles and gun. Like some of the Sukhoi and MiG fighters you'll face when the balloon goes up, the Tomcat is perhaps more effective than the F-16 at long range. Nobody, nobody fights better at close range.

The preceding is a hypothetical account of the kind of real air-to-air engagement being fought every day by the fast fighters of stateside Tactical Air. In wartime, many of these squadrons would "chop" (roughly, transfer) to combat commands overseas, such as US Air Forces in Europe or Pacific Air Forces.

The F-16 Fighting Falcon is not just spectacular in looks, style and performance. It's rapidly becoming the most important western fighter of the second half of the twentieth century— an immortal, worthy of mention in the same breath as Spad, Mustang, Sabre and Phantom. As many as 4,000 have been built or placed on order already,

Out in the wilds of Colorado, specifically at Peterson Field in Colorado Springs where Bob Greby handles his camera, F-16C 84-0255 of the 312th Tactical Fighter Training Squadron puts in an appearance. The blade antenna on the dorsal fairing is a distinctive feature of the C and D models. *Robert B. Greby*

The 157th Tactical Fighter Squadron in South Carolina was the first Air National Guard outfit to convert to the F-16A Fighting Falcon. The squadron was wearing an SC tail code for a time but seems to have dropped it of late, while the large billboard for the Palmetto State is new. Carrying ordnance colored blue to denote its practice status, plane 79-0295 is working out at Nellis AFB, Nevada, during a Gunsmoke tactical weapons meet in October 1989. *David F. Brown*

meaning that the Falcon has a chance to exceed the 5,100 airplane production run of the F-4 Phantom or even the 7,200 run of the F-86 Sabre. In a nation no longer quite so assured about being on the leading edge of technical know-how, the F-16 is evidence that Americans can design, build and fly a truly outstanding airplane.

A former Phantom outfit, the 347th Tactical Fighter Wing at Moody AFB, Georgia (MY tail code), was one of the final active-duty units to convert to the Fighting Falcon. F-16A 83-1094, wearing the wing commander's colors and hooked up to umbilicals, is seen at Gunsmoke, Nellis AFB, Nevada, in October 1989. *David F. Brown*

25

Tactical Air

It's peacetime. We're a vast nation of spacious skies and wild blue expanses. We're a people who say we dislike war. More than we might realize, we're confronted with one heck of a problem figuring out how to rehearse fighter pilots for the real thing.

The fighter pilot is a fiercely competitive being who thrives on challenge and needs to be tested to the outer limits. A virtuoso in a fighter cockpit needs practice that is genuinely realistic. His problem is like that of the M1 Abrams tank driver who can practice realistically only by driving into a house and allowing it to collapse around him, creating a "hide": not too many homeowners are ready to volunteer their dwellings.

The fighter pilot needs to have his talents sharply honed. In plain English, he needs space to practice in. Hopefully, our fighter pilot is also going to have the very best fighter plane the American taxpayer can give him.

When Tactical Air Command was formed in the lean, postwar years, equipment was hard to come by. The Air National Guard squadrons that support TAC have lived an especially spartan life since available funding for new jet fighters had to be earmarked for "regular" units. The Texas Air National Guard was among many state militia units that employed the F–51D Mustang, the prop-driven fighter that excelled in World War II and Korea. This restored Mustang is visiting Langley AFB, Virginia, on 11 June 1977. *Robert F. Dorr*

Each generation of fighter pilot learns that his isn't just a glamor job with good flying and plenty of fun, rather, that he's going to have to strap in, haul down the canopy, take off and fight.

As a country we haven't always been ready when war came knocking, nor have we been exempted from paying a painful toll when we weren't. At Pearl Harbor, when Lt. George Welch defied the odds by struggling aloft from Wheeler Field in a decrepit P-40 and shooting down four Japanese attackers, we weren't ready to fight. Today, we try. We try very hard. Those F-4s, F-15s and F-16s inscribing vapor trails up against the top of the atmosphere, or threading their way through canyons at breakneck speed, are flying under conditions as true-to-life as we can make them. But we face two critical problems struggling to keep our Tactical Air pilots combat-ready. The problems are money (how to pay for it) and realism (how to simulate war in peacetime).

And they're not new.

Tactical Air Command was established on 21 March 1946 and moved its headquarters to Langley Air Force Base, in the Virginia tidewater, on 1 May 1946. The first commander of TAC was Maj. Gen. Elwood R. (Pete) Quesada, a respected World War II fighter group commander. With a brief interruption, 1948-50 during restructuring, TAC has grown to become the overseer of the Air Force fighter community in the United States, a kind of holding company which has never fought a war itself but keeps men and machines ready to go elsewhere to fly and fight.

Today's TAC takes in interceptor squadrons that once belonged to Air Defense Command (ADC), also formed on 21 March 1946, at Mitchell Field, New York, with Lt. Gen. George B. Stratemeyer at the

helm. By 1961, ADC had become the largest command in the Air Force with an incredible 109 fighter squadrons. When the Soviet threat shifted from bombers to missiles, ADC declined and went out of existence in 1980. Its mission to intercept bombers and cruise missiles was shifted to TAC. Later, in 1985, this job was placed under TAC's First Air Force.

Air Force Reserve (AFRes) fighter squadrons in the United States are "gained" by TAC upon activation. AFRes boss Maj. Gen. Roger P. Scheer said in 1989, "The combat readiness of [the Reserve's] 58 flying squadrons has never been higher." The importance of the Reserve was highlighted the following year when the Reserve's 944th Tactical Fighter Group at Luke Air Force Base, Arizona, re-equipped with factory-fresh F-16C and D airplanes identical to those going to the regular Air Force. The Reserve includes five F-4 and two F-16 squadrons.

The term National Guard was devised by the Marquis de Lafayette, founder of France's *Garde Nationale,* during his 1824 visit to the New York Organized Militia. Air National Guard (ANG) squadrons are the flying component of the state militia and "belong" to the governor of their state until called up for federal duty, at

The jet age arrived for TAC and for the Air Defense Command, which then carried out the air defense mission, in the 1950s. Air National Guard and Air Force Reserve fighter pilots operated every jet that came off the line and moved quickly to the "century series" of supersonic jets which began with the F-100 Super Sabre. F-100D 55-2793 (foreground) in Vietnam-era T. O. 1-1-4 camouflage, belongs to the 110th Tactical Fighter Squadron, part of the 131st Tactical Fighter Wing, Missouri Air National Guard, located at Lambert-St. Louis International Airport *MO ANG*

The once-mighty air defense forces that guarded the United States from a bomber attack made effective use of the F-102A Delta Dagger. Not readily visible to the naked eye is the "wasp waist" or "area rule" effect introduced on the F-102A: by pinching the rear fuselage, the aircraft was able to operate more effectively in transonic regimes. By 1 September 1977, F-102A 55-3366 had been relegated to the status of gate guard at Hickam AFB, Hawaii. *Robert F. Dorr*

which time they are gained by TAC. In repeated major crises—Korea 1950, Berlin 1961, Vietnam 1967—civilian Guardsmen were called to active duty. For the air-to-ground mission, today's Guard has six F-4, three F-15 and five F-16 squadrons. For the air defense, or interceptor, job, the Guard has five F-4, two F-15 and six F-16 squadrons.

In this volume, we use the term Tactical Air to cover TAC (including former ADC), Guard and Reserve squadrons and their Phantoms, Eagles and Vipers. The challenge facing Tactical Air in the United States is to train and rehearse the violent art of fighting and defeating the enemy

The F-5E Tiger II remained a part of the Tactical Air's fast fighter force until 1990 as Aggressors aircraft. The F-5E is rarely photographed with its nosewheel strut hiked upward (to increase its angle of attack for takeoff) as seen at Carswell AFB, Texas, on 8 March 1986. Unfortunately, there is a sad footnote. Says the photographer Brain C. Rogers, "Old friend Capt. Todd Spangler was flying '05' that day. Todd separated from active duty a few weeks [later], became a full-time alert pilot in the F-4 Phantom with the 171st Fighter-Interceptor Squadron, Michigan ANG, and shortly thereafter was killed in a tragic traffic accident while pulling alert. . . ." The F-5E finally left tactical air's inventory when the last Air Force examples were transferred to the Marine Corps in 1989-90. *Brian C. Rogers*

when no enemy is in sight and no threat seems terribly pressing.

Our streets fester with evidence that we do not abhor violence as much as we claim. But an adversary in a fighter jet is farther away, more abstract; we find it difficult to think of fighting enemy aircraft as "real." The F-15 and F-16 interceptor pilot may actually see a Soviet Bear bomber on rare occasion (see chapter 4) but to most of us, a Russian or Libyan MiG is no more real than the cardboard cutouts in a Clancy-style techno-thriller. And war doesn't seem real, either, not a real prospect. We catch TV sound bites about peace breaking out in every locale from Romania to Mongolia. The F-16 crews who deployed to the Persian Gulf in Operation Desert Shield in August 1990 became the first in a generation to fly missions under warlike conditions.

We want to tell the young lieutenant in an F-16 cockpit to keep up his situational awareness. We want to hone his instincts, so that if the real thing comes he'll be the best there is. But we can't concentrate on turning out the world's best fighter pilot if we're distracted by citizens complaining about airport noise, or

The man in the cockpit—men, in the two-seaters—are the be-all and end-all of what the fighter business is about. These men (and women) need the best airplane the taxpayer can give them, adequate space in which to wring it out and realistic conditions under which to rehearse flying and fighting. These Idaho Guardsmen in a Phantom wear the new, lightweight helmet which is camouflaged, unlike the pure white "bone dome" of the Vietnam era. Yellow and black straps above the headrest are an alternate pull for the ejection seat, the primary trigger being a handle between the knees. At Boise International Airport on 23 May 1989, this pilot and back-seater are going through equipment checks before taxiing out. *Jim Benson*

32

The F-15A Eagle brought to TAC a big, powerful air superiority fighter. The 57th Fighter Weapons Wing (WA tail code) at Nellis AFB, Nevada, develops tactics and doctrine for each fighter type in service and performed early evaluations with the Eagle. The wing also runs a highly sought-after graduate course to turn out the Air Force's weapons instructors—pilots taught techniques not learned elsewhere—who then spread their knowledge among fighter wings. Plane 75-0042 is seen at Nellis in January 1977 in Air Superiority Blue, a color scheme that was employed briefly until replaced by Compass Ghost Gray as the standard F-15 color today. *Robert F. Dorr*

about low-level flying, or about sonic booms. And we can't do anything right until we stop feeding the bottomless stomach of the budget monster.

Our public debt is like the reptile who hides under your bed and comes out only at 3:00 a.m. You may be asleep but he's real. Everything about flying jet fighters—types of aircraft, the ordnance hanging under their wings, the number of flying hours—is affected by cost. In 1990, the biggest problem confronting Americans was not Saddam Hussein but our inability to pay our way in life. This challenges

Long after Eagles and Falcons were joining the older birds in the fast fighter aviary, the stalwart F-106 Delta Dart continued to soldier on as the principal interceptor employed in defense of the American heartland. The 106 served with Air Defense Command before ADC was taken over by TAC in 1980; it served with Air National Guard squadrons after the regular Air Force decided—temporarily, as it turned out—that interceptors weren't that important. One pilot flew F-106s from 1961 to 1981—a twenty-year career in this one aircraft type. Aircraft 59-0155 is a two-seat F-106B model of the New Jersey Air National Guard, which was the very last F-106 outfit and only recently converted to the F-16A. *Jim Benson*

the readiness of our Tactical Air fighter force at its core.

We're reminded, always, of the cost of the hardware. TAC wanted to keep its squadrons of Aggressor fighters to simulate Soviet MiGs in real-as-life ACM (air combat maneuver) training. And TAC wanted a "Wild Weasel" replacement for today's F-4G Phantom which has the unique mission of taking out an adversary's SAM (surface-to-air missile) sites. A Rockwell version of the European Tornado has been proposed for the latter job and would make a spectacular sight in US markings. But today's fighter pilot will almost certainly be sent into some future battle without the benefits of Aggressor training or Weasel support. Both were axed from the budget in 1990.

It's belt-tightening time. Less obvious is the cost of small parts, the thousands of little wires, bolts, snaps and gizmos that go into our airplanes. Lt. Col. John J. Harty, until recently maintenance chief of the 110th Tactical Fighter Squadron in St. Louis, points out the difficulties of maintaining a fleet of F-4E Phantoms the newest of which are approaching twenty-five years of age: "You can no longer find a supplier for some items in the airplane. Some companies which built components of the F-4E are not longer in business."

We tend to think of the F-15 and F-16 as the newest and snazziest things in the sky. Some are. But for perspective, note that in 1990 early F-15A Eagles were found vulnerable to wing spar cracks, having reached the fifteenth year of their twenty-two-year service lives. Where basic design is concerned, none of our fighters has been around for less than twenty years. Yet in World War II, fighters were designed, tested, flown, served in combat and retired from service, all in the span of four to five years. The

36

Soviets still produce a new fighter every four to five years. So age, like cost, is one of those realities facing the men who fly fast fighters.

One of Gen. Robert D. Russ's priorities on taking command of TAC in May 1985 was to solve a shrinkage of supplies and replenishment spares for the Pratt & Whitney F100 engines used in F-15s and F-16s. The engine spares problem seemed well in hand five years later and having a second powerplant, the F110 from General Electric, provides some diversity. More attention is needed, today, to "things under wings" if an edge in air-to-air combat is to be maintained. Scheduled to depart his key role in October 1990, General Russ can point to many achievements—this is one.

The AIM-9P, latest version of the heat-seeking Sidewinder, is considered state of the art even though the basic design of this air-to-air missile is more than thirty years old. The AIM-7M Sparrow radar-guided missile, once used only by the F-4 Phantom, is of increased importance now that its "shoot 'em in the face" capability is being added to the air defense version of the F-16A for the interceptor mission. But it's time for the Sparrow to be supplanted, then replaced. The "fire and forget" AIM-120A AMRAAM (advanced medium-range air-to-air missile) was scheduled to

For many years, camouflage was de rigueur in the Tactical Air community, the ultimate version being this wraparound lizard green, also known as Europe One, on F-4E Phantom 68-0353 of the 347th Tactical Fighter Wing, Moody AFB, Georgia. The use of a braking parachute is standard when landing the Phantom. By contrast, because its wing provides a ground cushion effect on final approach, the F-15 Eagle is not equipped with a brake chute and does not need one. The 347th is another unit that converted to F-16s. *Jim Benson*

In due course, the Phantom took on the same gray coloration as the Eagles and Falcons that joined it in the fast fighter world. When it was still being flown by the Oregon Air National Guard's 142nd Fighter-Interceptor Group, before conversion to the F-15A Eagle, F-4C Phantom 64-0776 at least had a small touch of color provided by its battle stars, the three red stars which denote MiGs downed by this Phantom in Vietnam. On the boom of a KC-135 on 3 August 1989, 64-0776 now wears the coloring which seems destined to be the final paint scheme for the Phantom in operational service. *Jim Benson*

When the F-16 joined the force, it was seen as a kind of "hot rod," having begun life as the winner of a lightweight fighter design competition. Like many of us, the F-16 gained some weight as it grew older, but it remains the most nimble and agile of air combat fighters. F-16A 80-0544 belongs to the 31st Tactical Fighter Wing at Homestead AFB, Florida. *Jim Benson*

come on line as this volume was in preparation, but is taking longer than originally planned.

The man in the cockpit is everything. Today's captain, representing the "average" F-15 pilot—age twenty-five, married, one and a half children—is likely to have 700 to 900 flying hours in his aircraft and to have had forty to fifty ACM engagements. In the future, he'll get ACM experience with fighters from other squadrons as the Aggressors are phased out. An almost invaluable tool to this pilot is the Flag exercises run by TAC.

Best known of these is Red Flag, derived from Southeast Asia experience, which began as a fighter-versus-fighter contest. Red Flag has been expanded to include diverse aspects of tactical fighter training in a very large, combined exercise which rehearses air crews against simulated

F-16As 81-0751 and 81-0666 fly over southwestern Montana on 18 August 1989. Especially noticeable on the aircraft on the right is a pitot tube located three-quarters of the way up the leading edge of the vertical fin. This is the sort of thing that sends modelers swinging from trees. It is what the Air Force calls a vertical taillighted floodlight, used for improved visibility during AAR (air-to-air refueling). Because the item is understood to be a TCTO (Time Compliance Tech Order) kit, it is found on some F-16As, such as these of the Montana Guardsmen, but not on other F-16As, such as the Falcons at Andrews AFB. *Jim Benson*

It is doubtful that we shall ever again see an Oregon-based Eagle as colorful as F-15B 76-0139, which went to Portland's 142nd Fighter-Interceptor Group replete with state name, missile-carrying Hawk, and group designation plastered across its tail. In more recent times, 76-0139 has been toned down to various shades of gray. In this view taken shortly after delivery, an electrical grounding wire is visible trailing from the lower rear of the aircraft. *Jim Benson*

enemy ground and air opposition. Simulated SAMs, known as Smokey Joes because of their realism when fired, are employed together with realistic anti-aircraft guns. As many as

250 aircraft fly up to 4,200 sorties during each six-week Red Flag exercise, seven of which are held in one year. The sun-drenched American desert at Nellis Air Force Base, outside Las Vegas, makes a colorful backdrop for British Tornados, French Jaguars and Korean Phantoms as allies join American participants.

Less well known are Green Flag, devoted to electronic warfare, Blue Flag, which tests battle management skills, and Checkered Flag, which trains TAC crews in overseas deployment. In the 1950s, it was possible for entire squadrons, even wings, to deploy overseas *en masse* to expose pilots and personnel to realistic

conditions. In the 1990s, the price is too high and deployments must be made on a selective basis.

The USAF Air-to-Air Weapons Meet, nicknamed William Tell, is the semi-annual test of air defense capabilities, pitting F-4, F-15 and F-16 interceptors (and participants from other services) against QF-100 and QF-106 target drones.

The realism of Flag and William Tell exercises notwithstanding, training with live ordnance is costly and infrequent. An AIM-7M Sparrow missile, for example, is priced at $740,000 and the crew of the F-4, F-15 or F-16 routinely goes for a year or more without ever firing one.

Dummy missiles used to simulate the Sparrow (and others) use electromagnetic impulses, but "firing" a signal is not the same as firing a shuddering, smoking rocket. Tactical air planners work constantly on ways to enable crews to achieve more practice with live rounds.

The final reality of the fighter-pilot business is that our nation is running out of room. Vast mountain ranges and amber waves of grain are the stuff of song. But just at the very time a typical fighter mission requires more cubic miles of sky than ever before, we are becoming more crowded and more cramped. Like the traffic gridlock that paralyzes our

suburbs, bumper to bumper airplanes in some regions make it downright impossible to practice in fighters under warlike conditions.

For realism, a fighter sortie must include a thorough wringing out of the entire mission profile—takeoff, cruise, ingress, battle, egress. The ranges where we fly simulated combat were more than large enough when we had slower, shorter-legged airplanes. Today, the ranges are cramped and further pressures are imposed by noise and crowding requirements. The fighter pilot needs his space.

As we move rapidly toward a new century, and toward a new generation of advanced technology

fighters (ATF)—if, indeed, we get the ATF—the Tactical Air's fast fighters will have to remain effective despite all the problems, able to carry out their mission in a world of stealth, electronic warfare and all manner of high-tech weaponry. Most of the success of Tactical Air will have to be credited to the almost incredible dedication and skill of the people of the fighter force. The support and understanding of the citizenry will help as our F-4, F-15 and F-16 people prepare for fighter operations in the twenty-first century.

Phantoms Forever

Biggest. Fastest. Most powerful. Most expensive. The list of superlatives for the F-4 Phantom runs on and on. The Phantom was—we would like to say *is,* but the past tense is apt—the standard against which every fighter of its era was judged. Everything else in the air had to contend with the almost impossible challenge of defeating the Phantom, and nothing ever did.

It's touching to watch a Phantom two-ship of the 110th Tactical Fighter Squadron, Missouri ANG, taxiing out from the confined space available to this squadron, wedged into a cramped corner of Lambert-St. Louis International Airport—an airport it shares not only with airlines but with the corporate giant founded by the enterprising James S. McDonnell, builder of the Phantom. Loyal members of the 110th, doubtlessly

Triple MiG killer. This F-4C Phantom 64-0776 shot down three MiGs in Vietnam, earning the trio of red stars painted on its air intake splitter plate. Armed with live AIM-7 Sparrow radar-guided missiles (in under-fuselage bays) and AIM-9 Sidewinder infrared missiles (astride inboard pylons), this F-4C is cruising over southern Oregon on 3 August 1989. At this time, the 142nd Fighter-Interceptor Group, Oregon Air National Guard, was in the process of converting to the F-15A Eagle. The group's F-15As were coming from the 318th Fighter-Interceptor Squadron at McChord AFB, Washington, which was deactivating. *Jim Benson*

devoid of bias, will tell you that their Phantoms are the cleanest, best cared for and best flown machines on the airdrome. Some say that even today, retrofitted with 1990s radar, the Phantom could fly and fight with the best of them.

Like a high-strung filly under firm control, there is something about an airplane in the right hands. You can't see it. You can't quantify it. But when you watch those twin Phantoms in their Hill Gray Two camouflage turn at runway's end, light up and begin to roll with the noise from their J79 engines reverberating across the field, you *feel* that the pilots and back-seaters in those F-4Es have brought so much to bear in experience, knowledge and skill—and yes, love—that St. Louis's Phantoms in their final days are being flown at the edge of their envelope and can still compete with the F-15Es being cranked out by the builder across the field.

In St. Louis, most of the squadron's part-timers *work* across the field, manufacturing today's generation of jets. Which raises some interesting questions about whether St. Louis's 110th will ever re-equip with the (bleep) Lawn Dart. Everyone recognizes that the (bleep) F-16 is the fighter of the future for ANG units—there are no F-15 Eagles available for ANG squadrons that do not already have them—and, to be sure, the (bleep) company at least has a corporate headquarters in St. Louis. But at that airfield, where 5,068

Previous page

One of the last units in Tactical Air Command to fly the F-4E Phantom was the 4th Tactical Fighter Wing at Seymour Johnson AFB, North Carolina. One of the last Phantoms in the twenty-two-year production run was "block 62" airplane 74-1649, wearing the wing's SJ tail code during a visit to Dayton, Ohio, in September 1984. Note cylindrical fairing at leading edge of left wing, which houses TISEO (Target Identification System, Electro-Optical), a kind of electron-assisted telescope used to pick up the bad guys at long range. This aircraft carries two underwing fuel tanks on outboard pylons, and a baggage pod. Cockpit boarding ladder and grounding wire have been extended. By the advent of the 1990s, most Phantoms were no longer painted in this lizard green or Europe One paint scheme, having shifted to today's gray color. *David W. Menard*

Phantoms were manufactured and where the ANG has flown the plane for twelve years, if a fighter wasn't manufactured over on the other side of the runway, no matter how good it was, it would still be Brand X.

Until the Phantom, no fighter pilot willingly set forth to fly a "hot" combat aircraft with a second man taking up space and weight in the back seat. Fighter pilots were, and are, loners. To many, the idea of a two-seater simply runs counter to the aggressive spirit and individual flair that is so much the essence of the fighter pilot. Even Capt. Steve Ritchie, the first Air Force ace of the Vietnam period, agrees that a two-seat fighter was effective only if both crew members flew together constantly as a "hard" crew and, even then, only if both were highly qualified. That "extra baggage" in the back seat became less burdensome when airmen over Hanoi discovered the value of a second pair of eyes, a second opinion.

To quote back-seater Spike Devane, who flies with the Illinois Air Guard's 170th squadron, "If you're a back-seater, being in a dogfight, even a simulated one, is like trying to track ants on the kitchen table while you're in the living room with a pair of weak binoculars." The back-seater directs the pilot in an intercept. The best thing he can help with is to get as close to the enemy as possible without being seen. Devane continues, "If it's a bad day, he'll direct himself and the pilot to the eternal regions by pulling out in front of the enemy" and giving an opponent a clear shot.

No fighter wing commander ever happily leads his men into battle with an aircraft that is expensive, sophisticated, difficult to maintain and unforgiving. Ritchie was never able to understand why the main radio on the F-4 Phantom was situated behind an ejection seat, making it necessary to remove the unwieldly seat in order to achieve even the simplest transmitter repairs. Col. Robin Olds upbraided designers and denounced equipment every time an air-to-air missile should have worked and didn't. Yet when the chips were down, Phantoms scored most of the 198 MiG kills in Vietnam, racked up sixty or so elsewhere and came out on top nearly every time they were challenged.

The F-4 Phantom proved conclusively the value of a twin-engine fighter. Among fighters in the

In days when Phantoms were still camouflaged but helmets weren't—a curious omission since both the naked eye and an infrared missile can lock onto the helmets shown here—F-4C Phantom 63-7676, *Noio*, of the 199th Tactical Fighter Squadron, Hawaii Air National Guard, tooled around wearing two MiG kills. Unfortunately, the battle stars are unearned, for this particular Phantom never shot down a MiG. The caveat in chalk with check mark comes from arming crew and tells pilot to "check six"—that is, be alert to his six o'clock or direct rear position where a MiG might sneak in. *Peter Mancus*

world today, only the F-16 is very successful with one engine. The F-14, F-15, F-18, F-20, MiG-29, MiG-31 and Su-27 have twin engines. The F-4 was initially produced without a gun—almost certainly a mistake—but all fighters today are gun-armed.

When the Phantom replaced the Republic F-84F Thunderstreak with the 12th Tactical Fighter Wing at MacDill AFB, Florida, on 5 December 1963, the *Tampa Times* proclaimed that "probably never again will the Air Force buy another one-seater fighter plane. . . ." Three decades later, this assessment about the superlative Phantom seems to have been premature. Today, MacDill is home for the 56th Tactical Fighter Wing which provides much of tactical air's F-16 training. While F-16B and F-16D two-seaters are fully combat-capable, they represent less than ten percent of the Viper force. The back-seater is out of a job.

In 30 January 1990 sunshine on the crowded hardstand at St. Louis, paired red stars adorn another MiG killer, F-4E Phantom 68-0338. Front canopy rail bears the name of the brigadier general who commands the Missouri Air Guard's 131st Tactical Fighter Wing. The internal 20 mm M61A1 cannon unique to the F-4E model is located between the lower jaw of the shark's teeth and the somewhat awkwardly shaped nosewheel housing. *Robert F. Dorr*

In the break. F-4C Phantom and MiG killer 64-0776 of the Oregon Air National Guard (its red stars absent from the right side of the aircraft) snaps away in a sharp bank and shows us just how heavily armed a Phantom can be. Though this version was built without an internal gun, this F-4C carries a 20 mm Gatling gun in SUU-23/A dispenser beneath the fuselage centerline. In addition, the Phantom carries four all-white AIM-7 Sparrow radar-guided missiles in bays beneath the fuselage and four AIM-9 Sidewinder infrared missiles beneath the wings. *Jim Benson*

At Andrews AFB, Maryland, when the F-4D Phantom gave way to the F-16A/B Fighting Falcon in the 127th Tactical Fighter Squadron, District of Columbia Air National Guard, the most poignant event in the transition was the formal ball for the WSOs (weapon system officers) who had been key members of the team for a decade. At St. Louis, Terre Haute and other locations where Phantom squadrons remain, WSOs are viewed as an almost priceless human

Next page
F-4C Phantom 63-7530 on 3 August 1989, displaying the now-defunct Air Defense Gray paint scheme, which included provision for much larger national insignia on the upper wing than is normally carried by a fighter. Aircraft 63-7530 is approaching a KC-135 tanker and has opened up its dorsal receptacle for the tanker's "flying boom" refueling probe. The all-gray radome is an anomaly. *Jim Benson*

resource. Some have been flying the airplane since its earliest days. Many have between their ears institutional memory which is veritably a national treasure.

Apart from a couple of chase airplanes in California, no Phantoms fly any longer in the active-duty Air Force. In the Air Force Reserve, the transition to newer equipment is proceeding but it's unlikely that any Reserve airplane will ever be as well cared for as one F-4 Phantom that belonged to the 465th Tactical Fighter Squadron at Tinker Air Force Base, Oklahoma. A Phantom at Tinker that had downed two MiGs in Vietnam was kept in tiptop shape by a crew chief who made an avocation of studying the history of MiG kills. Other MiG-killing Phantoms (including aircraft 64-0776, which graces these pages) have ended their flying careers and are on display on poles from Portland to Dayton to Niagara Falls. But the existing force of Phantoms forges on.

There are alive today young men and women for whom the F-4 Phantom is a first airplane and who, even now, view the Phantom as the standard against which all other fighters must be measured. But the Phantom's air-intercept radar, once the best in the world, does not have the range or accuracy of newer radars. Its cockpit, once viewed as spacious and roomy, has become increasingly cluttered with retrofitted items of equipment, especially for the back-

Another MiG killer, seen on 15 July 1989, is F-4D Phantom 66-7661 of the 121st Tactical Fighter Squadron, DC Air National Guard, at Andrews AFB, Maryland. When the F-16A Fighting Falcon came along to replace the Phantom at Andrews, 66-7661 was set aside for restoration and will soon be displayed on an outdoor pylon. *Robert F. Dorr*

seater, and is not as comfortable as newer ergonomic cockpits.

Too, the Phantom has a rather large RCS (radar cross-section)—though no more than the F-15 Eagle—and many Phantoms still have engines that emit long smoke trails, advertising the location of the F-4 in a fighting environment where stealth means success.

Young pilots flying Phantoms today were not around when the aircraft was developed in 1957–60 as a fleet defense interceptor for the US Navy. They were schoolchildren when the Phantom became a brute of a fighter-bomber and earned a title no aeronautical designer ever covets—that of "multi-role" fighter. Today, after combat in several wars including fighter-versus-fighter action as the world's premier MiG killer, the Phantom has reverted to its original role and many of those still in service are now interceptors (see chapter 4).

An F-4D Phantom like those flown by the "Happy Hooligans," the 178th Fighter-Interceptor Squadron, North Dakota ANG, stationed at Hector Field in Fargo, is powered by two 12,440 lb. thrust afterburning General Electric J79-GE-17 turbojets and is equipped with the partly solid-state APQ-109 radar. Our typical F-4D was designed to carry AIM-4D Falcon missiles, but the Falcon was never popular so a typical load today comprises four Sidewinders, four

In another view that emphasizes the crew, the all-important human element that makes a fast fighter what it is, St. Louis's F-4E Phantom 68-0351 prepares to run up on the hardstand. The one-piece windshield, found on only one other Phantom in inventory, is readily apparent. Hose from auxiliary power unit (APU) is also visible, as is crew ladder which is used by both crewmen. The back-seater must then clamber over the engine intake and squeeze into the rear cockpit. *Robert F. Dorr*

Another view of the since abandoned Air Defense Gray paint scheme, here in sunsplashed Hawaii on 29 July 1984. F-4C Phantom 64-0851 has since been retired to that Great Boneyard in the Sky, but for many years *Boa 'E Ula* and colleagues flew from Hickam AFB and defended our only island state. *Robert F. Dorr*

Sparrows and (at times) a centerline gun. For the back-seater especially, this Phantom's cockpit is now severely cluttered, visibility is no longer what it once was and comfort is at best an elusive goal.

The D model of old "Double Ugly," also called the Rhino, is soon to disappear from inventory. The E models will be only a few years behind, the F-4E Phantoms with an internal M61A1 20 mm Vulcan, or Gatling, cannon. Our Phantom-oriented friends in St. Louis may have to change their mission and convert to the RF-4C photo-reconnaissance

ship—scheduled to be around much longer—if they really want to avoid transitioning to the (bleep) F-16.

We have mentioned, and will keep mentioning, the budget and the high cost of maintaining Tactical Air's fast fighter force. Because the 1990s arrived as a time of fiscal uncertainty, it could not be said for certain that the final F-4 Phantom mission would be logged at any time in the decade, or even that the Phantom would be out of service in the predictable future. Past or present tense, the F-4 Phantom remained—remains—a class act and a tough act to follow.

Yet another in our arcade of MiG killers is F–4D Phantom 66-7551 of the 89th Tactical Fighter Squadron, Air Force Reserve, stationed at Wright-Patterson AFB, Ohio. The absolutely pristine, mirror-like surface of the nose radome tells us a little about how Reservists and Guardsmen take pride in the appearance of their fast fighters. Based on research by Air Force Museum expert Tom Brewer, it was learned only in 1990 that 66-7551 actually didn't shoot down two MiGs—the crew given credit for the kills was flying a different jet that day. But now that F–16s are flying in Dayton and 7551 is on display. The red stars are still part of its attire. *Robert F. Dorr*

TX for Texas, it says on aircraft 74-1630, one of the very last F-4E Phantoms manufactured for US forces and belonging to the Air Force Reserve's 704th Tactical Fighter Squadron, Bergstrom AFB, Texas. Seen at the 1989 Gunsmoke exercise at Las Vegas, this E model Phantom wears a camouflage paint scheme which is unique to this squadron and has never been seen with any other unit. *David F. Brown*

Interceptors

Bear country. Far up into the North Atlantic, high above the curvature of the planet, the air itself seems frozen with flecks of ice that glint in the cold, cruel sun. Tricky and dangerous winds howl across flat, boggy, treeless plains until the tundra gives way to cold, open sea speckled with ice floes, bergs and vast reaches of emptiness. But the air is not empty. A huge object is out there, coming on relentlessly.

A huge glint of silver, freakishly large, too large to have been placed there by nature, is coming on with primeval force: the Soviet Bear-H bomber, which seems to command the polar sky. No, it is not a reconnaissance aircraft and, no, its mission is not to take pictures. Still in production after thirty-five years, it is the only swept-wing turboprop warplane ever to see service. The massive Bear-H is practicing its very purpose for existing—a doomsday attack on North America. Tucked in its cavernous silver bomb bays, the Tupolev Bear-H carries four nuclear-tipped cruise missiles capable of being

The Bear. A blur in motion when viewed through the hand-held camera in the hands of an F-4 Phantom back-seater, this Soviet Tupolev Bear-B symbolizes the threat to North America that requires a strong interceptor force. Military leaders make their plans based on a potential enemy's capabilities, since they cannot discern his intentions, and perestroika has not reduced the need for readiness. *Alan Miller*

The "Happy Hooligans" of the North Dakota Air National Guard, at Fargo, fly the oldest F-4D Phantoms in service and used them as part of the Creek Klaxon deployment to stand guard at Ramstein, Germany. When Soviet aircraft, including the vaunted MiG-29, were shown off at Abbotsford, Canada, in August 1989, a Soviet pilot was given a ride in the back seat of a "Hooligans" F-4D, like aircraft 64-0949 seen here. A generation of real and Walter Mitty fighter pilots may have known the Phantom as the best of the best, but the Russian was unimpressed. Said he, "The cockpit resembled a steam ship." *Don Logan*

launched a thousand miles from their target—the American heartland far to the south.

"I'd like to splash him," Purvis thinks aloud. Purvis is Lt. Col. Robert C. (Septic) Purvis of the 102nd Fighter-Interceptor Squadron, Massachusetts Air National Guard.

How do you intercept an enemy rushing toward North America with intent to do harm? Air defense against "atmospheric vehicles," a Pentagon term to encompass bombers and cruise missiles, gets full-time attention from plenty of people, including high-ranking generals. But on this bruising wintry day in 1988, a bare 660 miles from the American coast, the defense

It would be almost impossible to describe how much airmen loved the F-106A Delta Dart interceptor, which served in air defense units from 1959 to 1988. Built around the 24,500 lb. thrust Pratt & Whitney J75-P-17 afterburning turbojet, the F-106A was linked via its complex and bulky MA-1 electronic fire-control system through a digital data link into the nationwide SAGE (semi-automatic ground environment) system. A real "queen of the skies," to quote pilot Lt. Col. Jack Webb, the F-106A was also the last American aircraft built solely for the interceptor role. These Montana ANG 106s are taxiing at Malmstrom AFB near Great Falls. *Jim Benson*

of North America passes from the Top Brass to a very junior, blue-suited officer. It all comes down to Purvis, leader of TARMAC Flight, a formation of two F-15A Eagles stationed at Otis Air Force Base, now forward-deployed at Loring Field, Maine, on 27 July 1988.

"Let's do this smoothly," urges Purvis over the radio.

"Two's in," says the pilot in the second F-15A. Following air-intercept procedure, TARMAC 02 is purposely hanging back about three miles, the second F-15A pilot maintaining an IR (infrared) fix on the Bear-H. If the Russian bomber displays hostile intent or its gunners open up on Purvis, TARMAC 02 will kill the bomber with an AIM-9 Sidewinder IR-guided missile.

A second flight of two F-15A Eagles, callsigns BASELEG 01 and 02, loiters several miles in the background, orbiting so that their forward progress occurs at the same speed as the Bear's. If necessary, the second pair of Eagles will engage with AIM-7 Sparrow missiles.

Purvis eases back his throttle, tucks his F-15A in at a high angle of attack, and cruises alongside the mighty Russian bomber. Beneath his oxygen mask, the F-15A flight leader grins with satisfaction. "We've got him cold," says Purvis, close enough to the Russian bomber to see its rivets.

In October 1987, F-15A Eagle 76-0021 of the 5th Fighter-Interceptor Squadron looms over Jim Benson, who had better hope the Eagle jock has no reverse gear. This F-15A was preparing for a cross-country flight to Loring AFB, Maine, where the 5th was temporarily standing alert—during which time Eagles intercepted two Soviet Bear bombers flying recon off the Atlantic coast. The 5th was later deactivated in 1988, so these markings appeared only briefly on F-15As. *Jim Benson*

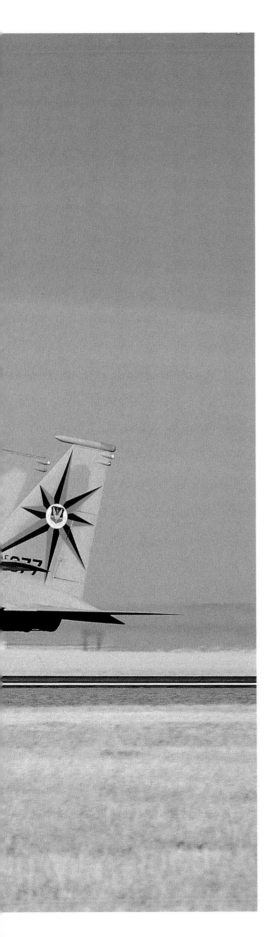

In Tactical Air squadrons that operate the fast fighters of this volume, the opportunity to see a *real* Soviet aircraft comes rarely. TAC's Eagle-equipped 57th Fighter-Interceptor Squadron at Keflavik AB, Iceland—the only part of our TAC, ANG and AFRES community located outside the United States—routinely looks at Bears and other Soviet "biggies." Others get the chance far less often. When the Vermont Air Guard's 158th Fighter-Interceptor Group, launching from Burlington in its F-16s, intercepted a Bear-D on 1 March 1990, it was only the thirty-first "contact" since the unit was assigned interceptor duty three years earlier.

But if real-life air encounters do not happen often (in the encounter just described, the Bear and its AS-15 cruise missiles quietly proceeded on their way), Tactical Air's fast fighter community prepares for the real thing day after day, night after night, in good weather and bad. F-4 Phantoms, F-15 Eagles and F-16 Fighting Falcons are ready—some of them on short-fuse alert—if the real thing ever comes. The interceptor job is overseen by Tactical Air Command's First Air Force, commanded in 1990 by Maj. Gen. Richard A. Pierson (the other two numbered air forces in TAC, the Ninth and Twelfth, divide up other responsibilities).

If a war were to come to American soil, the interceptors of TAC's First Air Force and of the Air

National Guard (as well as those of Alaska Air Command) would chop to the commander-in-chief of the North American Air Defense Command (NORAD), who at the time of this writing is Gen. Donald J. Kutyna. The fighting role of these interceptors would be dictated from NORAD's well-known redoubt at Cheyenne Mountain near Colorado Springs.

Eighty-five percent of the metal—that is, the airplanes—of the stateside interceptor force belongs to Air National Guard squadrons, gained by TAC in peacetime, NORAD in war. Guardsmen are superb pilots, radar operators and mechanics. Only a few of them labor full time; most hold jobs elsewhere and are dubbed "weekend warriors." Few Guardsmen are fond of the term and can claim with some accuracy that their aircraft, their talents and their dedication are superior to those of the regular Air Force. Because they are so dedicated, joint exercises frequently end up with the Guard's men and women atop the score sheets, ahead of the regulars.

At the onset of the 1990s, many Guard interceptor squadrons are still equipped with the F-4 Phantom. The versatility of these flying outfits is dramatically illustrated by the story of the Creek Klaxon exercise, a story that could at first glance seem dated but is, in fact, as new as tomorrow's possibilities.

An unusual overseas movement of ANG interceptors, Creek Klaxon took place between April 1986 and April 1987. A composite force of F-4D Phantoms from three Guard squadrons deployed to Ramstein AB, Germany, to stand alert while the regular Air Force wing at the base stood down for the purpose of converting from F-4E to F-16.

One squadron of the Ramstein wing normally handles the air defense or Zulu Alert mission in West Germany. For a full year, the job was

With tires smoking, an F-15A Eagle from the 318th Fighter-Interceptor Squadron, McChord AFB, Washington, lands after a two-hour mission in November 1987. The distinctive markings of the 318th are a throwback to the glory days of the long-defunct Air Defense Command. With its long-range and Sparrow capability, the F-15A makes a superb interceptor. *Jim Benson*

71

taken over by the Air Guard's Phantoms which stayed on five-minute alert ready for any Soviet bombers that might cross into NATO territory.

Creek Klaxon officially got under way on 7 April 1986 when US Air Force Chief of Staff Gen. Charles A. Gabriel announced the successful completion of an Alert Force Readiness Inspection which enabled the Guard Phantoms to go to work. Air crews pulled alert duty with an average of two to three live scrambles per week. As quoted by historian John M. Deur, a typical exercise was described by Lt. Col. Raymond Klosowski from the 148th Fighter-Interceptor Group of the Minnesota Guard: "When the horn goes off, we're out of the alert barn at 100% military power. We hit the corner at around 60 mph and take off. Doing this while heavily-armed (four AIM-7 Sparrows, four AIM-9 Sidewinders and a centerline SUU-23 gun pod) creates quite a strain on the ol' Phantom."

The F-15 Eagle is often described as the first fighter designed with participation by pilots. In the interceptor role, the F-15 evokes thoughts of strength and of sheer size—big plane, big engines. On the ground, the F-15 Eagle stands considerably higher than other fighters and the pilot has a sense of being on top of the world. In flight, the great

Two F-15A Eagles of the 318th Fighter-Interceptor Squadron prepare to take off to fly mock air-to-air combat with F-16As of the 120th Fighter-Interceptor Group, Montana Air National Guard in November 1987. Even though their principal mission is to detect, intercept, identify and (if necessary) destroy intruding bombers and cruise missiles, interceptor pilots never cease to practice their air-to-air skills against other fighters. *Jim Benson*

size of the airplane is accompanied by great power although, again, with a large radar cross-section.

F-15A Eagles are driven through the air by two 23,930 lb. thrust F100-PW-100 turbofan engines which enable the aircraft to get up to 1,653 mph in clean condition at altitude. A foot shorter in length than a DC-3 transport, the F-15A employs APG-63 radar to locate targets as distant as 100 miles.

Years ago, air defense leaders coined the acronym DIID as a shorthand term for the job they're faced with—detect, identify, intercept and destroy. A few experienced air defense experts still argue that an interceptor should have a radar operator in the back seat. A ground-controlled intercept, they argue— climbing to ambush a bomber or cruise missile using vectors and other information provided from the ground—involves a considerable amount of "busy work" and is too much for one crewman. While a single-seat Eagle is undeniably effective, two men will more than double its effectiveness. These are the voices crying for a future interceptor based on the F-15E, the two-seater originally conceived solely for the ground interdiction role.

The F-16 Fighting Falcon now outnumbers other fighter types assigned to the interceptor mission. When the F-16 won the Air Force's lightweight fighter competition in 1972 and became standard in NATO air forces, it was seen as a highly maneuverable, relatively light and simple fighter with considerable air-to-ground and air-to-air capability. Its role as an interceptor in the defense of North America came years later. The F-16A is powered by a single 23,840 lb. thrust afterburning F100-PW-100 turbofan, with the F110 available as an alternative. In clean condition it can knife through the skies at 1,350 mph. Eventually, all F-16s will acquire the AIM-120 AMRAAM advanced missile which will be linked with the programmable APG-66 radar for stand-off intercept capability.

The Fighting Falcon exists in several versions of the F-16A model alone. F-16As with the Montana Guard have a pitot tube protruding from the upper leading edge of the vertical fin, while F-16As with DC Guard at Andrews AFB, Maryland, do not. The new version known as F-16A ADF (air defense fighter) is being remanufactured for the interceptor mission. The first was turned over to the 114th Tactical Fighter Training Squadron, Oregon ANG, located at Klamath Falls. The principal difference of the F-16A ADF is that it uses the radar-guided AIM-7 Sparrow. Outwardly, it can be distinguished by a device once found on all interceptors for which the need seems obvious—a searchlight for night intercepts, located behind the pilot on the port side of the fuselage.

F-15A Eagle of the 318th Fighter-Interceptor Squadron at "last chance" inspection before taking off from McChord AFB, Washington, to fly and fight. At last chance, pilots raise their hands and show them to the ground crew to demonstrate that they are not in a mode to accidentally drop ordnance which could injure ground crewmen working beneath. *Jim Benson*

This striking portrait is of F–15A Eagle 79–054 of the regular Air Force's Alaskan Air Command (AAC). Note "Big Dipper" band on inside of vertical tail. The 43rd Tactical Fighter Squadron, part of the 21st Tactical Fighter Wing, operates from Elmendorf AFB, Alaska, but is seen here on a visit to the Lower Forty-eight. Tactical Air Command's jurisdiction covers the forty-eight contiguous states but does not include Hawaii or Alaska, where Guard aircraft fall respectively under PACAF (Pacific Air Forces) and AAC. *Jim Benson*

F-15A Eagle callsign STING 21 on the boom of a KC-135R Stratotanker during a refueling mission. This is another Elmendorf-based Eagle of the 21st Tactical Fighter Wing. *Jim Benson*

These Eagle fighters of Portland's 142nd
Fighter-Interceptor Group fly high above
Pacific breakers on 31 January 1990. *Jim
Benson*

Assigned to the air defense mission, although not yet equipped to carry the AIM-7 Sparrow radar-guided missile, F-16A Fighting Falcons 80-0565 and 81-0751, flown by Maj. Mark Meyer and Capt. Ray Lynn, bore along over Flathead Lake in northeastern Montana on 18 August 1989. Aircraft on right has a Sidewinder missile in an unusual position, since infrared AIM-9 missiles are normally carried on wingtip launch rails. *Jim Benson*

Who Are Those Guys?

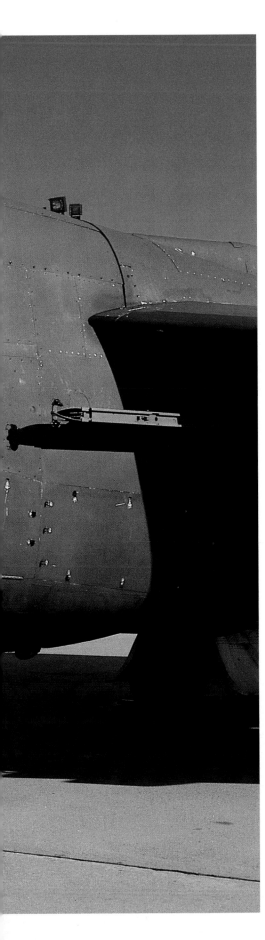

Out in Las Vegas where slot machines jangle, the divorce industry thrives and the sun always shines—most of the time—the big business is fighters. At Nellis Air Force Base, eight miles northeast of town, they've been wringing out F-4s, F-15s and F-16s over the desert for a generation. Nellis's 57th Fighter Weapons Wing carries out development work that enables fast fighters to use their cannons, bombs and missiles in combat. And a hundred miles north at Tonopah Range, they've been flying the F-117A stealth fighter, which is just out of the closet.

At Nellis on 13 October 1989, a surprisingly chilly day for fighter workouts over the desert, the best in the business is the 169th Tactical Fighter Group, an F-16A Fighting Falcon outfit from the South Carolina Air National Guard. To those guys, the Air Force's Tactical Gunnery and

Thirty-one A-7K twin-seaters were acquired for conversion training and Stan/Eval (standards and evaluation) duties. The A-7K is fully combat capable but differs from the A-7D in having half the ammunition for its gun and a slightly longer takeoff run. Aircraft 80-0288 of the 149th Tactical Fighter Squadron, Virginia Air National Guard, at Richmond, on 17 February 1990, is rarely seen out of doors, even when all "buttoned up" with red warning labels. The encircled kangaroo at rear canopy identifies Dave Hudson, the Virginia Guard's Australian-born flight surgeon. *Robert F. Dorr*

Bombing Competition, called Gunsmoke, is a cakewalk.

Gunsmoke pits sixteen teams of five aircraft each from the TacticalAir community in simulated air-to-ground work which includes delivering six BDU-33 practice bombs onto a bullseye target, low-level strafing against a mock enemy tank, and a low-level misson with four 500 lb. Mark 82 retarded bombs against a simulated enemy airfield. Each of these missions involves an actual combat profile, navigation over "enemy" terrain and overcoming defenses. Mere participation in the Gunsmoke contest—the Indy 500 of air-to-ground—is a coveted prize for the best of the best.

And somebody has to be the best of the participants. This year, the 169th flew the demanding combat profiles in its F-16A Fighting Falcons and racked up the Top Team trophy for the 1989 competition. How'd they do it? "We functioned as a team,"says Maj. George (Jet) Jernigan.

An Air Force Reservist, Capt. Pat Shay of the 944th Tactical Fighter Group, Luke AFB, Arizona, racked up individual honors as the Top Gun of the competition by flying and fighting in *his* F-16C Fighting Falcon better than anybody else.

Yes, it's true. The F-16A has an air-to-*ground* mission. Our book is a celebration of air-to-air, but this chapter belongs to those *other* guys, the mud movers.

The South Carolina Air National Guard's 169th Tactical Fighter Group was the first Guard outfit to equip with the Viper. F-16A 79-0304 with Sidewinders on wingtips bores a hole in the sky trying to catch up with the 169th's previous airplane, A-7D 72-0258, in obsolescent "wraparound" camouflage. Tactical Air gets double duty out of the F-16A which is assigned to squadrons having both air-to-air and air-to-ground responsibilities. *Don Linn*

The Tactical Air community gets headlines and Hollywood interest from air combat. But we can't secure peace or win any war without the (sometimes not very) fast fighters which exist for the purpose of bringing ordnance down on targets on the ground.

The attack guys, the mud movers, are vital to the Tactical Air mission. They fly the A-7D Corsair, the A-10 Warthog, the F-111 Aardvark and the F-117A stealth fighter.

The A-7D—to be technical, the Air Force never formally picked up the Corsair II nickname applied to Navy versions—is perhaps the least appreciated of all Tactical Air assets and is universally nicknamed the Sluf which, in polite translation, means Short Little Ugly Fellow.

Except for a few test ships, all Slufs are now assigned to Air National Guard squadrons. They tasted the real thing during Operation Just Cause, the US invasion of Panama in December 1989. In early fighting, A-7Ds came under fire while flying support missions. A detachment of the 180th Tactical Fighter Group of the Ohio

Warthog. One of Tactical Air's tank killers basks in the sun at Biggs airfield near El Paso, Texas, on 5 October 1985. The BD tail code identifies this Air Force Reserve A-10 as belonging to the 917th Tactical Fighter Group, stationed at Barksdale AFB, Louisiana. *M. J. Kasiuba*

Blue Thunder, an A-10 Warthog, fires its 30 mm GAU-8 cannon. An A-10 loitering at 280 mph can engage a tank at a distance of 10,000 feet and fire a 30 mm round which will reach the target in just three seconds. The cannon will split open a T-72 or T-80 tank from that distance, at least double the range of 20 mm cannons found on other US warplanes. *USAF*

ANG, under Lt. Col. Charles Vaughn, bore the brunt of this effort. Air National Guard A-7Ds flew seventy-six close air support sorties and fired 2,715 rounds of ammunition.

Driven through the air by a 14,250 lb. thrust TF41-A-1 turbofan engine without afterburner, a version of the Rolls-Royce Spey 168-62, the A-7D was never intended to be very fast, isn't, and can reach Mach 0.88 or 698 mph at sea level only on a very good day. "Speed is life," pilots say over the modern battlefield, and the A-7, like its comrade the A-10, has only enough of it to give the pilot a little comfort. But many believe that the Sluf was ahead of its time and still has an important place over the battlefield today.

Boeing four-engine fighter? In fact, this particular version of "Who are those guys?" is not a fast fighter or a member of the Tactical Air community at all, but gains status as a kind of honorary fighter plane by virtue of inclusion in these pages. The authors traveled extensively to fighter bases throughout the United States. At every stopover, they were reminded to give credit to the unsung heroes of tactical air—the Strategic Air Command tanker crews who provide the "fill-up" in mid-air that gives a fighter its legs. In-flight refueling has become so much a part of routine that it could easily be taken for granted, but it should not be. Boeing KC-135R Stratotanker 62-3533, a re-engined KC-135A, belongs to the 301st Air Refueling Wing and is seen in July 1989. *Jim Benson*

Aardvarks eternally. Many of the men who strap into the swing-wing F-111 Aardvark are not among the limited few still on active duty who flew the aircraft in combat in Vietnam and Libya, but all sing the praises of the huge, complex, costly and aging F-111. In the distant past, there was discussion of F-111 units re-equipping with the F-15E Eagle, but this is no longer a realistic prospect. Pilot and WSO (weapons systems officer) of an F-111A belonging to the 389th Tactical Fighter Training Squadron, Mountain Home AFB, Idaho, go through pre-flight checks on 23 May 1989. *Jim Benson*

In the "air to mud" mission, the name of the game is precision delivery of ordnance. The A-7D introduced a new standard of accurate navigation and bomb delivery. Its navigation/weapon delivery system frees the pilot of most of the constraints imposed by manual bombing, augments his ability to find targets and permits attacks from arbitrary maneuvers. The system includes tactical computer, inertial measurement set, Doppler radar system and forward-looking radar. The Projected Map Display Set (PMDS) gives the pilot an actual map, its motion coinciding with that of the

aircraft. Much of this paraphernalia is primitive by the standard of today's glass-cockpit digital airplanes, but when the Sluf came into existence in the mid-1960s, it was revolutionary.

Going into the 1990s, fourteen Air National Guard squadrons were equipped with the A-7D and each also had at least one two-seat A-7K. The manufacturer was flight-testing two test ships dubbed YA-7F, the upgrade of the Sluf for the 1990s. The YA-7F is powered by the F100 afterburning engine and can use the F110, the same powerplants as the F-16 Fighting Falcon, and also has a HUD and instruments similar to those

of the F–16. Though no firm plans existed to produce the YA–7F, the miserly funding climate of the early 1990s made it a low-cost alternative to newer, big-budget aircraft. One problem: with a fifteen-inch fuselage "stretch," the YA–7F was a mite too "long" to retain the Sluf nickname.

The Sluf was replaced in Tactical Air outfits by the ungainly, slow-flying A–10. Thunderbolt II, the Air Force wanted to call it. Everybody calls it the Warthog. It's unique, a warplane created for the sole purpose of bringing a heavy cannon to bear against tanks. Not a bad idea when

American forces are confronted by massive numbers of main battle tanks in on the European plains and the Korean peninsula.

Tactical Air's A–10 Warthog force is divided among three TAC fighter wings, five Air National Guard squadrons and four Air Force Reserve groups, as well as two outfits overseas. The A–10 is squared-off and box-like in its contours, lacking curves meant to please the eye, and it is surprisingly large—about the size of a World War II B–25 Mitchell bomber, from which it borrowed a twin-rudder tail. It's driven through the air by a pair of rear-mounted 9,065 lb. thrust

An F–111A of the 366th Tactical Fighter Wing coming in for a landing at the end of the day, 23 May 1989. The variable geometry wings are in the swept-forward position for best lift during low-speed airfield pattern work. Glove vane located behind engine inlet serves as a speed brake to further improve low-speed handling characteristics. TAC badge on the vertical fin is located just below a slanted formation light, known to some as a "slime light" because of the greenish hue it emits after dusk. *Jim Benson*

TF34-GE-100A turbofans. Built by a company no longer with us (the plant that turned out A–10s is now a credit card collection facility), the lizard

The real thing . . . a real Aardvark, with real bombs. Pretty as a picture on the ramp at Mountain Home AFB, Idaho, this F-111A has CBU (cluster bomb unit) dispenser on inboard pylon and four 500 lb. Mark 82 bombs on each outer pylon. The latter swivels to maintain its location relative to the airflow when the variable geometry wing of the F-111A is being moved to the sweptback position. Though it looks like a posed PR shot, this is in fact a view of a real F-111A getting ready to make a delivery to the bombing range. *Jim Benson*

green A-10 exists for the purpose of carrying aloft its 4,029 lb. GAU-8/A Avenger seven-barrel Gatling-type anti-tank cannon firing a 30 mm depleted-uranium round.

The A-10 can engage a T-54 or T-62 tank at 10,000 feet and split it open with cannon rounds. "I can hide in the trees, pop up, and kill him before he knows I'm there," says Dan Kuebler, an Air National Guard A-10 pilot. To fight against the contours of the earth, masked from the other guy's radar and infrared, A-10 pilots possibly do more low-level flying than anybody else. "They say speed is life, and everybody admits that ours is the slowest fighter in the Air Force," says Kuebler, "but we live down on the ground and we have the tactics to defeat armor." Other missions, such as close-air support, make the A-10 more versatile than is generally acknowledged. But killing tanks is the be-all and end-all of the A-10. With airframes piling up more and more flying hours and logistics support becoming harder and harder to keep up, the A-10 may have a limited future.

If a YA-7F advanced Sluf *is* eventually ordered into production,

Head-on view of Aardvark at Mountain Home AFB, Idaho, 23 May 1989. *Jim Benson*

A-7s might end up replacing A-10s, which replaced A-7s to begin with.

The air-to-ground mission is also the business of the Aardvark, the mighty F-111 fighter-bomber that proved itself in Vietnam (after initial problems) and paid a visit to Libya's Colonel Khaddafi a few years ago. The F-111 is vivid illustration of the variety of warplanes that are called fighters and which serve in tactical fighter squadrons. A heavyweight compared to the A-7 and A-10, the Aardvark is really a bomber. But watch out. *This* bomber has a gun and can tote a couple of Sidewinder missiles. While the F-111 is moving mud, it can also make trouble for any MiG trying to interfere.

Braving the chill at Mountain Home AFB, Idaho, to observe the F-111 in its lair, one of the coauthors watched the Aardvark howl to life and spring aloft with a load of four Mark 84 1,000 lb. bombs, heading out on a long-range mission. This is the only Tactical Air warplane that routinely borrows the use of the Strategic Range Training Complex, a vast area of Montana, Wyoming, Colorado and South Dakota brimming with Soviet emitters and mock SAM sites, routinely used by B-1B and B-52 bombers for practice. The F-111 is in many ways more like those strategic bombers than the Phantoms, Eagles and Vipers in the tactical community.

"Our mission normally is to hit targets deep behind the lines," says

Starting up the Sluf. At Byrd Field in Sandston, Virginia, where low-key A-7Ds replaced thundering F-105s in the 1970s, pilot takes a cue from T-shirted crew chief on how to crank up aircraft 69-6198, also known to Virginia Air Guardsmen as *Dollar Ninety Eight*. The glass-covered fairing beneath air intake holds a Pave Penny laser designator. *Robert F. Dorr*

Col. Arnie Franklin, deputy for operations of Mountain Home's 366th Tactical Fighter Wing. "We can travel hundreds of miles, use our navigation and delivery system to pick out a target the size of a pin prick, and put our bombs right on it. Give me a tanker and I can go anywhere in the world, hit anything." With the F-111, as with other air-to-ground warplanes, precision of ordnance delivery is the name of the game.

The F-111 is also one aircraft in our Tactical Air community that remains the exclusive province of the regular Air Force; it has yet to reach Air National Guard or Air Force Reserve units. An expensive, unique airplane that is costly to support, it probably never will. Two F-111 wings serve with TAC within US boundaries—at Mountain Home and Cannon AFB, New Mexico—and two are abroad. Each wing is equipped

Outdated ground attack camouflage Mark I and Mark II: The hard-working A-7Ds of the Pennsylvania Air National Guard demonstrate Vietnam-era T.O. 1-1-4 camouflage (the two aircraft in the foreground) and lizard green, alias Europe One (left background). The latter paint scheme can still be widely seen but is now being replaced by gray. The airplanes themselves always seem to last longer than the thinking that dictates airplane colors. *Don Linn*

with a different version—F-111A, F-111D, F-111E and F-111F—which have slightly different powerplant, avionics and internal systems. TAC was scheduled by the end of 1991 to acquire forty-eight more Aardvarks, which were formerly the strategic forces's FB-111A, with the new designation F-111G.

The F-111 is powered by two 18,500 lb. thrust TF30-P-3 turbofan engines and crewed by a pilot and weapons systems officer. That second crew member is an unsung hero, jokingly called a YOT (for "you over there") but taken very seriously for his duty of getting the warplane and its bombs to the target. The F-111 has a nuclear capability but is viewed as an American national treasure because of what it can do with conventional bombs: carry out strikes in Third World environs like those in Operation El Dorado Canyon, the April 1986 bombing of terrorist-related targets in Libya. A fully loaded F-111 can weigh over 100,000 pounds. At low levels, maximum speed is typically around Mach 1.2 or 910 mph.

At one time, the Air Force had hoped to replace the erstwhile Aardvark with the F-15E Eagle, which equips just two wings in Tactical Air's fighter force. For many years the latter was billed as the F-15E Strike Eagle and publicized as

With afterburners lit, an F-111A of the 366th Tactical Fighter Wing thunders down the Mountain Home, Idaho, runway at sundown on 23 May 1989. Even on burner, the Aardvark is not as loud as some tactical aircraft, but Mountain Home officers consider themselves fortunate to have a supportive community that doesn't seem to mind the sound of freedom. Flying at night is a better approximation of the F-111A's wartime capability than a sunny-day mission. *Jim Benson*

95

That's Pennsylvania Dutch country down there, and PT signifies Pittsburgh. The lizard green A-7D Corsair II, number 70-1049, belongs to the 146th Tactical Fighter Squadron, Pennsylvania Air National Guard. *David F. Brown*

the only version of the "Fifteen" with mud-moving responsibilities. By 1990, the F-15E seemed to have acquired a new image and was being billed as "dual role"—equally adept at both air-to-air and air-to-ground missions. Despite the change in emphasis, F-15Es are bombers just as F-111s are bombers.

"Odd man out" in our celebration of the air-to-ground aces of Tactical

Air is the F-117A stealth fighter equipping the 37th Tactical Fighter Wing, commanded by Col. Tony Tolin and scheduled in 1992 to move from Tonopah to Holloman AFB in Alamogordo, New Mexico. Incorporating technologies designed to foil enemy radar, infrared and visual detection methods, the F-117A results from a "black program" about which almost nothing was said publicly for

more than a decade. Not particularly fast, not a carrier of vast amounts of ordnance—though it's a bigger airplane than is generally understood—the F-117A exists solely because of its stealthiness.

In the Panama operation in December 1989, two F-117As dropped bombs intended to stun the defenders at Rio Hato airport in the moments preceding a parachute assault by American Rangers. Four more were roving Panama checking known hideouts of leader Manuel Noriega who, unfortunately, was at a location not known to US intelligence. The Panama effort showed how the F-117A can be employed, at considerable expense, for a precision effort against a high-value target. Because it is designed to decapitate an enemy by lopping off his command and control facilities, the F-117A has been called a "blinder": a precision strike in the right place will leave the enemy sightless.

The last of fifty-nine F-117A aircraft was apparently delivered in July 1990. The F-117A is increasingly in the public eye, though it probably will not be seen, soon, at a Gunsmoke competition!

Eagles Evermore

The crew chief leans over you in the cockpit and snaps the final clamp, completing the process of securing you in the ejection seat of your F-15C Eagle. Your first impression is one of size. Adorned with the FF tail code of the 1st Tactical Fighter Wing (First Fighter), your Eagle is indisputably a very large fighter aircraft. The wing stretches out into the distance, making you wonder if visibility will be adequate. Thumbs up, the crew chief signals. He pats your lightweight helmet and scrambles down the internal boarding ladder. You're in the F-15C Eagle cockpit, high up, on your own.

"PLUMBLINE 02, you're cleared to taxi," says a voice from the tower.

You reach runway's end and turn to take off. The sun peeks up at 5:50 a.m., on a frigid February Tuesday at Langley AFB, just outside Hampton, Virginia. Capt. Don Ellis, in the other F-15C Eagle, is going to be your target today and you're going to "attack" him. The intent is to give you one more stage of ACM (air combat maneuver) practice on the "building block" principle. You'll make a high-speed vertical attack from below with a chance to use missiles but you're going to work very hard to achieve a "gun solution." Eagles in some squadrons draw the job of intercepting bombers, but in the First Fighter the business of the day is killing MiGs.

You fire up the big fighter at "last chance," running through your checks. "PLUMBLINE 01 and 02 are clear

for takeoff, two-ship formation," comes over the tower radios. You watch Ellis's aircraft, detect the tell-tale moment when his landing gear flexes just slightly and kick in your afterburner a split-second after he does.

Your Eagle, weighing 39,000 pounds, uses just over 2,800 feet of Langley's main runway, rotates at 120 knots and clears the concrete at 140 knots. The visibility is stunning: the entire Virginia tidewater laid out around you, the jumbled ticky-tack of Mercury Avenue in Hampton with its melange of neon, the brooding hulks of cruisers and aircraft carriers in port at Norfolk, splotches of urban growth wedged in by sea and bay. It is a brief transit to Range W386A, seventeen miles off the coast.

The biggest advance in the fighter business has been in the radar. Your F-15C is equipped with APG-63 radar and it's really something. First of all, it's a pulse Doppler radar. The Doppler means

F-15A Eagle 76-0094 of the 94th Tactical Fighter Squadron, part of the 1st Tactical Fighter Wing (FF for First Fighter) flying clean except for centerline fuel tank in September 1981. A second F-15A is virtually concealed by the first. The glare from the window of the photographer's KC-135 appears in this view: a photo from a companion F-15 would have less glare but TAC is the only major command that prohibits cameras in the cockpit. *Robert F. Dorr*

F-15A 75-0058 of the 128th Tactical Fighter Squadron, part of the 116th Tactical Fighter Wing, Georgia Air National Guard, taxies out from Dobbins AFB on 27 April 1988. Pilots who fly the F-15 view it as the greatest air superiority fighter of its age, but critics point out that, because of its sheer size and prominent jet intakes, the F-15 has a large radar cross-section (RCS) and is therefore vulnerable to enemy detection at great distances.
Donald S. McGarry

that it only senses things that are moving. And all that *clutter* on the scope—ground returns—is history, it doesn't appear. You get a computer-generated portrayal in clean form of what the radar is seeing. Unlike the radar on Phantoms and earlier ships, you don't have to tweak and tune. And you have look-down, shoot-down capability as well.

Visibility isn't *perfect* from the Eagle, though. There is a "low six"

(referring to the six o'clock position) blind spot and, of course, the space beneath the nose. But with the possible exception of the F-16, the Eagle has the best view of anything flying. Tactics call for using the aircraft in pairs as mutual cover, even in turns, so you can never be caught blind.

Over the range, you make some turns to reaccustom yourself to Gs. They say the Eagle doesn't routinely

Early in the career of the F–15A Eagle, aircraft 74–0083 of the 1st Tactical Fighter Wing ran into a minor in-flight emergency not far from home base, Langley AFB, Virginia. Just to be on the safe side, 0083 picked up an escort in the form of F-4J Phantom 153825 of Marine Corps fighter squadron VMFA–122, the "Crusaders," and made a landing at the nearest field, NAS Oceana, Virginia. The F–15 was still new and the F–4 still the Queen of the Skies when this happened on 20 October 1977. *Robert F. Dorr*

The now-defunct 318th Fighter-Interceptor Squadron belonged in the 1950s to ADC—once the largest command in the Air Force with over 109 squadrons. When TAC took over the air defense mission, interceptor squadrons acquired tail codes, such as the short-lived TC (for Tacoma) seen on F-15A 76-0093. Soon after the code was assigned, the squadron was deactivated, but meanwhile 0093 made this approach for landing at McChord AFB, Washington, with its giant "barn door" speed brake sticking up behind the cockpit. *Jim Benson*

"Fight's on," he intones. You manipulate stick switches—hands on throttle and stick, remember—and have a radar lock on him almost immediately.

When the F-15C's radar is locked on, you get locked-in with your head-up display. A little box appears on the HUD pointed exactly where the radar is aimed so that, in the whole sky, if you've got a radar lock-on, you look through HUD and right into your little box and—lo and behind—the enemy is right there. If you lock him up before he's within visual range, when he does get in visual range— bam!—he's inside that little box.

The other F-15C Eagle is nineteen miles away, thirty degrees to

Next page
An Eagle in its prime—F-15A 77-0109 of the 142nd Fighter-Interceptor Group. This view accents the muzzle aperture for the 20 mm M61A1 Vulcan, or Gatling, cannon at the leading edge of the right-hand wing root. Various orifices pocking the structure of the F-15A use airflow to cool internal systems, while small round fairings at each wingtip contain ECM (electronic countermeasures) aerials. *Jim Benson*

the left. "Fox one," you say. It's the standard call meaning that you've launched an AIM-7F Sparrow radar missile. Today is just pretend, but if you *had* launched a real missile you'd be getting vector information on your

HUD while the Sparrow bores at the other guy.

Today, Ellis in PLUMBLINE 01 is not doing much to evade. You'll get practice against a wily and determined enemy—but first, you'll build up practice points against a pilot who isn't testing you too hard, who's just flying around.

Following through with the pre-briefed plan for this mission, you apply throttle and burner, climb sharply, bank at 18,000 feet and turn straight into Ellis's path of approach. The APG-63 display shows him coming at you at about ten miles now, another 10,000 feet higher up. Your second weapon is the heat-seeking AIM-9M Sidewinder. The M model, unlike early Sidewinders, doesn't need to get an infrared lock on Ellis's exhaust. It is an all-aspect missile and can engage him from the front. You

At the 1988 William Tell competition, the biannual world series of the fighter-interceptor business, ground crew members load AIM-7M Sparrow radar-guided missile aboard F-15C 78-0478, which is visiting Tyndall AFB, Florida, from its home base at Kadena, AFB, Okinawa. Numerous warning flags, most of them hanging from AIM-9 Sidewinder infrared missiles, deliver the same message as the red air intake cover. This Eagle is not quite ready to fly, just yet. It will fly, though, and engage a QF-100 target drone while not merely the pilot but the ground crew as well is graded for achievement. *Robert A. Pfannenschmidt*

Next page
Whatever else may be said about the F-15 Eagle, from this angle it clearly has no competitor for graceful and aesthetically pleasing lines. STING 21 and STING 22, a pair of F-15Cs wearing the AK tail code of their Alaska Air Command connection, are pausing for fuel while working out in an air-to-air contest with Montana Air Guard F-16As, 14 September 1989. *Jim Benson*

The First Air Force is Tactical Air Command's fighter-interceptor outfit, and the 48th Fighter-Interceptor Squadron, Langley AFB, Virginia, was its first Eagle-equipped squadron. Aircraft 76-0126 was one of the first Eagles assigned to the air defense mission and is seen during a visit to Nellis AFB, Nevada, on 2 April 1987, wearing the plumes of the boss, Maj. Gen. Buford D. Lary. The distinctive blue-white tail stripes harken back to an earlier era when air defense units wore brilliant colors. *Brian C. Rogers*

pull your turn, line him up and call, "Fox two."

HOTAS. You're able to keep your head up, trying for the visual on Ellis. As they say, Lose sight, lose the fight. So what is your hand doing? The switch under your thumb has three positions. One says, I want to shoot radar missiles (Sparrows). Another is for heat-seeking missiles, the third for the gun. When you move that switch, it changes all of the modes in the radar associated with shooting whichever piece of ordnance you've selected. So if you select the gun, and you happen to have the radar in eighty-mile scan mode, it shifts immediately to ten-mile scope.

Today, you haven't really fired a Sidewinder. Ellis is about to pass you, overhead. Now you're pulling G,

At Luke Air Force Base near Glendale, Arizona, F–15C 80–0062 of the 405th Tactical Fighter Wing taxies out, carrying an AIM–9 Sidewinder infrared missile which is colored blue to indicate a practice round. The Eagle's centerline fuel tank gives the appearance of being dangerously close to the ground—it holds 600 US gallons of 2,270 liters—but, in fact, there is no way the tank can be nudged against the ground. The pilot sits in an ACES II ejection seat which, when used, ignites in 0.3 seconds and can have the pilot outside, in the open, dangling from a fully opened parachute—even after ejecting from zero speed, zero altitude—in 2.3 seconds. *Brian C. Rogers*

109

trying to corner around for a gun shot. Your thigh-constricting G-suit tightens abruptly. Using a combination of feel and HUD cues, you come out of the turn and—you've missed him.

Yanking and banking in a twenty-ton metal cocoon four miles above the Atlantic requires practice, practice, practice. Capt. Don Ellis lights his burner, sending back that characteristic plume of red-orange flames from his twin burner cans. He heads out to sea—to pose as your enemy again. This time, he goes out only to a mile or so. This is gun range. You begin turning again, looking for a solution that will put your pipper on his Eagle.

"I'm in guns now," you say.

If Ellis—or an aggressive MiG-29 pilot—were to hit *you* with cannon fire, you'd have a better chance to live than pilots of past fighters. The Eagle isn't fly-by-wire like the F-16, isn't an Electric Jet, but all of the Eagle's hydraulic lines have return pressure sensing so that if the normal 3,000 psi that's going out comes back at, say, 650 psi (because a cannon shell has blown one of your lines open), the system, in effect, slaps a tourniquet on that part of the aircraft by shutting off the hydraulics in that sector. The rest of the hydraulic system survives—and works.

You go for Ellis again. You dump Gs in a turn going for the gun solution. Even well in visual range, he's not that easy to lay eyes on. His

With incredible symmetry, F-15C Eagles line up on the ramp at McChord AFB, Washington, on 14 September 1989, the sun glinting on their canopies. It was not recorded how well Capt. John Corrigan did when these Alaskan Eagles went aloft to do mock battle with Montana Guard F-16As, but the low-key presentation of the pilot's name is in keeping with the Air Force policy of toning down aircraft markings. *Jim Benson*

Eagle, like yours, has smoke-free engines and there are no contrails at this height today, so his Compass Ghost Gray Eagle is difficult to see with your Mark One Eyeball as it speeds over the gunmetal-gray Atlantic.

"Fox three," you say. If you were really firing the 20 mm cannon, it would make a smooth, humming sound, in split-second bursts. The muzzle flash behind you to the right is neither distracting nor blinding. Firing at rates up to 6,000 pounds per minute, the gun draws ammunition from a 940 round drum in the central fuselage, the belt passing above the engine inlet duct.

Today, there is no war, no MiG, only Ellis, insisting loudly (there is no way to prove it either way), "You didn't get me." PLUMBLINE 01 and PLUMBLINE 02 come together in the sky, form a two-ship and head for home.

The Eagle is the only one of our Tactical Air fast fighters with twin vertical fins, although the look is routine among the Tomcat and MiG communities. The *horizontal* tails work together for pitch and work differentially for roll, and at very high angles of attack you don't even use the ailerons for roll. You use the horizontal tails working in opposition. The electrical part of your hydraulic/electrical flight control system provides what it thinks is the optimum rudder associated with the aileron. You can literally fly with your feet on the floor and don't need to push on the rudder pedals.

You land your F–15C Eagle at 110 knots in a supporting cushion of ground effect and, with hardly any braking, easily make the first runway turnoff. While the Phantom uses a braking parachute with every landing to retard the sheer force and power of the heavy aircraft hurtling down the concrete, the Eagle does not have, or need, the chute thanks to the dynamic braking effect of the wing. The final act: you and Ellis stop briefly for a post-landing inspection by ground crew. Then, you taxi in and shut down.

The F–4 Phantom may be better known and the F–16 Falcon is already far more numerous, but the F–15 Eagle is a thoroughbred. You've been air-to-air in a jet that has flown to 103,000 feet and routinely hits Mach 2.3 at 40,000. In your ergonomic Eagle cockpit, you sit higher, fly faster. . . .

So much for another of the kind of real, air-to-air engagement being fought every day by Tactical Air's fast fighters. The airplanes are the best we can turn out, but it always boils down to the men. The F–15 Eagle pilot of today is clearly every bit as capable as the air aces of two world wars, of Korea, of Vietnam, who preceded him and set the standard to follow.

Crew chief of Alaska Air Command's F–15C Eagle guides his aircraft in to the blocks after a pilot "borrowed" it—the airplane "belongs" not to the throttle jockey but to the wrench twister—to fly a simulated air combat engagement with Vipers. The twin burner cans of the F–15C Eagle's exhausts look particularly impressive when seen from behind. In the air, this is *not* the view we want a MiG pilot to have. *Jim Benson*

Keeping the Peace

Their gear is down, like they're going to land. But they aren't going to . . . not yet.

With a deep-throated howl, the pair of low-flying jets emerges over the horizon and lines up for a low-level flyover of the main runway at Andrews Air Force Base, Maryland. Approaching above the trees, emitting black smoke in an era when most jet fighters are now smokeless, this pair of fast fighters flies as one aircraft, wingtip to wingtip, to create the sweetest, most beautiful two-ship formation your eyes have ever seen. The pilot of the lead F-4D Phantom, callsign BRAVE 32, is getting an opportunity for a pass over the main runway, a maneuver so ordinary, so routine, that he can do it almost without thinking. But today he thinks. Today is the last time.

Goodbye to lizard green camouflage and (probably) goodbye to aircraft with MiG kills painted on them. The 184th Tactical Fighter Group, Kansas Air National Guard, held its 31 March 1990 Phantom Out ceremony to mark the departure of the fabled Phantom from the unit that trained thousands of pilots and back-seaters. Earlier, on 7 July 1988, Brian Rogers's camera stopped F-4D Phantom 66-0271 of the Wichita-based fighter group's 127th Tactial Fighter Squadron, heading out on a mission. Flying in the back seat on this day was Lt. Col. Jim Bell who shot down a MiG in 1972 while flying a different Phantom also depicted in this book, F-4D Phantom 66-7661, which ended its career with the District of Columbia ANG. *Brian C. Rogers*

"I never fail to look up," says a mechanic.

At a busy airfield outside the nation's capital, the *president*'s aircraft can take off or land without attracting attention. All sorts of aircraft, of all services, come and go. Gorbachev has landed at Andrews. It is rumored, though it probably isn't true, that an F-117A stealth fighter made a landing at Andrews one dusky evening and no one was sufficiently aroused to take notice.

Well, maybe. But when a two-ship formation of F-4D Phantoms heads up-sun and comes across the concrete at 500 feet of altitude, it doesn't matter how inured you are, how immune you've become to the thrill, you *still* look up.

In the front seat of the second F-4D Phantom, callsign BRAVE 34, is a twenty-four-year-old first lieutenant. He has already qualified in the F-16A Fighting Falcon which replaces the F-4D in his unit. With a little luck, he'll still be flying fighters in the tenth year of the new century—turning Gs, yanking and banking in the F-22 or F-23. And he'll remember his brief stint in the Phantom the way you remember going to the museum when you were a kid.

"Okay," says BRAVE Leader, "let's do this real nice."

Three of the four men in this pair of F-4D Phantoms will not do it again. The end has finally come. On

Previous page
Single-seat and two-seat Viper in the pattern. This F–16A and F–16B typify the fast fighters that will equip Tactical Air's squadrons well into the 1990s and beyond. The "pimple" just behind the radome midway on side of fuselage is a radar warning antenna for highly sophisticated Fuzz Buster which tells the pilot when he is being strobed by hostile radar. The red light located just behind air intake is a forward position light used for routine navigation. The F–16 does not seem to require the navigation strip lights or slime lights carried by many other fighters. *Jim Benson*

31 January 1990, the 121st Tactical Fighter Squadron officially gives up its last Phantom. The newly arrived F–16 Viper does not have a work space for a GIB ("guy in back"). The weapons systems officer, WSO, as the back-

seater is formally known, is about to join the dinosaurs. "Roger that," acknowledges the WSO in lead's back seat. "Here we go."

BRAVE Leader is beginning to overshoot the runway in military power, cleaning up and pulling hard to left, when he ignites afterburner. With the gear coming up and long tongues of fire stabbing back from the Phantoms in one smooth, quick motion, it is as if some heavenly force has flicked the two Phantoms ninety degrees and thrown them at the top of the sky.

The sound of four afterburners is like a concussion. It shatters the sky and shakes the land. Yes, it is a legal maneuver, but it's loud; it's as loud as you can fly a jet fighter within hearing distance of taxpayers, and the sudden

On the hardstand at Kelly Air Force Base just outside San Antonio, Texas, F–16A 80-0559 of the 182nd Tactical Fighter Squadron gets ready to go on 3 September 1987. At the controls is Texas Air Guardsman Maj. Danny James. The pilot's father, Gen. Daniel (Chappie) James, was one of the nation's first black fighter pilots and rose to four-star rank. *Brian C. Rogers*

pull-up has sent the two Phantoms straight skyward.

BRAVE Leader levels off and precedes the young lieutenant around the pattern. Gear and flaps down again. This time, lining up on the runway, it will be a full-stop landing. BRAVE Leader heads out over those nearby woods and starts a descending turn. Bank angle, okay. Steady at 140

On 22 August 1984, when the 318th Fighter-Interceptor Squadron was still in the interceptor business, F–15A Eagle 76-0111 taxied out from a Detachment 1 alert barn at Castle AFB, California, for a very late afternoon summer mission. Nobody gets the pilot's attention more than the hard-working ground crewman who clears his aircraft for taxying and steers him around obstacles. The pivot fixing at the mouth of the air intake is in a lowered position here, obscuring the national insignia beneath the rear of the Eagle's cockpit. *Brian C. Rogers*

knots and twenty degrees angle of attack. Nose high.

The two Phantoms come in over the runway's end, settle to concrete

and pop their drag chutes. With the familiar, Phantom-like lack of grace, they settle forward and grind slowly toward taxying speed. BRAVE Leader takes the third turnoff from the main, taxies in and shuts down his Phantom for the last time.

"I have no words," he says, when asked about it. An era has ended.

Something old, something new. The business of flying fast fighters, and of upholding the preparedness that ensures peace, means getting rid of old Phantoms, working out with mid-career F–16As and F–15As, taking receipt of spanking-new F–16Cs and F–16Ds and—inevitably—looking forward to that

future F–22 or F–23 which is still way down the pike. No longer secret, the F–117A stealth fighter will attract some attention as it comes more and more into public view. But most transitions, most of the arrivals and departures that lead from the old to the new, are quiet and unpublicized. At Seymour Johnson Air Force Base in the North Carolina pine forests, a lot of people didn't even notice when the fabled 4th Tactical Fighter Wing began to transition from F–4E to F–15E.

As we approach that new century, the future of the fighter force is perhaps less clear than it has ever been. When this book was in progress

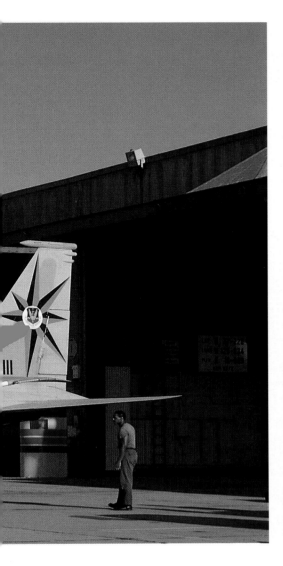

On 18 August 1989, a two-ship of F–16A Fighting Falcons continues its progress over the state of Montana. *Jim Benson*

it appeared that peace *was* breaking out all over, a phenomenon utterly unprecedented in world history. Saddam Hussein and Operation Desert Shield changed that view. But whether peace beckons or not, some kind of major spending cuts are inevitable. The future F–22 and F–23 are among possible candidates to be affected.

Some things, even in an era of uncertainty, can be predicted:

One, there will be some role for the F–4 Phantom for some time to

"One of my all-time favorite static views," says the photographer, Brian Rogers, who flies B–52s for a living. F–16A Fighting Falcon 79–0311 belongs to the commander of the 311th Tactical Fighter Training Squadron at Luke Air Force Base, Arizona, and basks in clean sunlight on 22 February 1986. One aircraft type employed by another branch of the armed forces is so notorious for leaking at its radome joint that it must be covered by a nose tarpaulin at all times while on the ground. The F–16A has no such problem and the appearance of the tarp, actually a petrochemical-based cover, would be rare even if the location were *not* the sunny Southwest. *Brian C. Rogers*

come, but the role is limited. When a proposal in the mid 1980s for an "upgraded" Phantom with new radar failed to attract the Tactical Air community, the future of the Phantom became finite. Although still capable of fighting and winning against newer fighters, the Phantom is sorely constrained by its radar—the best in the world in its time, but now hopelessly dated—and is becoming too expensive to maintain and operate. The drawbacks overcome the cost advantages of continuing to fly and fight with a dated machine.

Two, the F–15 Eagle is nearing the end of its production run, but is

Next page
Thirsty Vipers from the vast reaches of Montana hunker down to take on gas from aircraft 59–1445, a Boeing KC–135E Stratotanker, the E model being distinguished by the shape of its TF33 turbofan engines. A few tentative efforts at air-to-air refueling under operational conditions were successful during the 1950–53 Korean War, and flight refueling became almost routine—if there can be *anything* routine about whizzing through the sky in a steel cocoon—during the 1960–75 Vietnam conflict. The F–16A's capability to be refueled is routinely taken for granted in planning for mock combat missions. *Jim Benson*

More Arizona sunshine, to taunt those mortals who, like most of us, live in *real* weather. This F–15E Eagle, originally billed as the Strike Eagle, bearing serial 86–0186, is a factory-fresh item newly delivered to the 405th Tactical Training Wing when seen on 18 March 1989. Conceived as part of a superb engineering effort to be an air-to-ground version of the Eagle, the F–15E really possesses the dual-role capability with which it is more recently being credited in the manufacturer's brochure, and would be a problem for any MiG pilot lured into overconfidence. *Joseph G. Handelman, DDS*

nowhere close to an end to its career in Tactical Air. The final Eagle in American colors will probably be an F–15E ordered in 1991 and delivered two to three years later. Despite its new image as a dual-role fighter (after being initially touted as the Strike Eagle, or air-to-ground version of the F–15A/C), the F–15E is viewed in some quarters as too expensive. Some fighter pilots think they need more Eagles than they'll get.

Three, no other ship will challenge the F–16 Fighting Falcon as the fighter existing in largest numbers, with the longest and most lucrative future ahead. Perhaps partly by accident, the F–16 entered the world with enormous growth potential, so that new versions are coming along two decades after the initial design. Plans for a big-winged Agile Falcon version of the F–16 will produce, in effect, a second generation of Falcons

This *isn't* Arizona and the weather *won't* be featured in tourist literature, but the brooding clouds mark the conditions under which wars are fought. Taxying out are two F–15C Eagles, going aloft to show their stuff. The pilot sits unusually high off the ground in the Eagle and has excellent visibility while taxying. In the air, he has an almost unlimited 360 degree view. *Jim Benson*

likely to be in production well into the third millennium.

Four, the long-standing goal of forty tactical wings in the US Air Force is as dead as a MiG with a Sidewinder up its exhaust. Through the Reagan years and at the outset of the Bush era, forty wings remained "untouchable," the public target no policymaker in cost-cutting capital dared to tamper with. It now appears that Tactical Air's fast fighter force will be part of a thirty-three-wing force.

Other factors are less easy to predict, however, as fighter pilots prepare for the future:

One, the role of the F-117A Nighthawk stealth fighter not only isn't clear to outsiders, it may not have been fully decided by the Air Force itself. Committed to an unsuccessful effort to "get Noriega" during 1989 Panama operations (he was later "got" via other means), the F-117A is obviously intended to strike high-value targets. Today, the F-117A is much more in public view than previously, but its role in the larger scheme of things is not clear.

Two, the ATF (Advanced Tactical Fighter), which the Air Force will choose after testing two prototypes—the Lockheed YF-22 and Northrop YF-23—may or may not become the standard mount for a new generation of fighter pilots. Among hard funding decisions that must be made, the future of the ATF may be the hardest.

The Air Force has been doing its best to stick with ATF. Consider this news release:

"The Advanced Tactical Fighter (ATF) is the proposed air superiority fighter for the 1990s and beyond. The current generation air superiority fighter, the F-15, first entered the Air

Those Portland-based F-15A Eagles again, in another spectacular view of the fighters over the Pacific coast. *Jim Benson*

Force inventory in 1975. By the time the ATF begins to enter the force, it will have been more than two decades since the United States introduced the F-15."

Today, the ATF is alive and well. But in the halls of the Pentagon, in quiet whispers, a few Air Force officers are contemplating having to "make do" with improved Eagles and Falcons, passing over the next-generation ATF entirely.

At the same time, the armed forces face the most dramatic belt-tightening in recent history. For the first time since an all-volunteer force was created, many service members with fine records may have to leave involuntarily if the force reduction goals of the 1990s are to be met. Lt. Gen. Thomas J. Hickey states: "We've never messed over a bunch of people like we are about to do. It will take a generation to recover." Not the best climate to keep fighter pilots at their best!

Meanwhile, the fast fighters of the Tactical Air outfits are keeping the peace. It's not an easy job. It isn't always the most acceptable way to make a living, either. Long after being military became respectable again—as it did, belatedly, in the last decade—flying very loud warplanes at very low altitude continues to be a "community relations" problem.

It has been pointed out before. To remind people that management degrees and packaging skills are only part of the portfolio for an officer in shade 84 blue, a chief of staff ordered signs put up that told airmen, "The mission of the United States Air Force is to fly and fight and don't you ever forget it."

A less-direct version of the same message is a T-shirt showing an air-to-air missile on its way toward a MiG, subcaptioned with a slogan made famous by a phone company, "Reach out and touch someone."

127

The essential Eagle. It can have the kind of dark purpose suggested by this view. Or it can be a joy to fly, put through its paces in brilliant blue sunshine. The large size of the aircraft and its wing, which produce a large radar cross-section, is evident here. *Jim Benson*

The men who fly fast fighters know perfectly well that the old and sometimes corny words, the words like duty and patriotism, are still in the dictionary. Give them a Phantom, a Falcon or an Eagle to put through the wringer and these pilots will be ready. It is an old thought, a corny thought, but it remains as true as it ever was.

They *must* be ready. There is no other way to secure peace.

So far, with an occasional lapse, we have always managed to give the American fighter pilot the best possible leaders, organization and, above all, the best airplanes to do his job in. We'd better keep it up.

It still matters.